A Short Guide to the Films of Ozu

A Short Guide to the Films of Ozu

Doron B. Cohen

RESOURCE *Publications* • Eugene, Oregon

A SHORT GUIDE TO THE FILMS OF OZU

Resource Publications
An Imprint of Wipf and Stock Publishers
199 W. 8th Ave., Suite 3
Eugene, OR 97401

www.wipfandstock.com

PAPERBACK ISBN: 979-8-3852-7886-2
HARDCOVER ISBN: 979-8-3852-7887-9
EBOOK ISBN: 979-8-3852-7888-6

VERSION NUMBER 04/22/26

Contents

Notes to the Reader

All Japanese names are given in the Japanese order, that is family name first, given name second.

Macrons over some letters indicate a long vowel (ō, ū, ā).

Two consecutive i's should usually be read as a vowel followed by a consonant (for example: Kiichi = Ki-ichi).

The terms "pre-war" and "post-war" relate to the periods before and after the Second World War.

Introduction

Ozu Yasujirō (1903–1963) is regarded by many as one of the greatest masters of the 20th century cinema. He started working in the Japanese film industry at the age of nineteen, and began directing when he was twenty-four, continuing—with interruptions caused by the long war in Asia—almost until his death, which occurred on his sixtieth birthday. In Japan he was considered the "most Japanese" among film directors (whatever that means), and perhaps for this reason his work was not introduced to the world outside Japan until the early 1970's. However, cinema lovers all over the world were quick to recognize the universal qualities of his work, and were captivated by the humanism and beauty of his films, as well as by his unique artistic approach to film making.

What is the secret of the appeal of Ozu's films? Even after watching them many times, and reading much of what has been written about them, it is difficult for me to form a clear answer, perhaps because true art has an elusive quality that defies description, or requires very elaborate ones. Even on repeated viewing, these films can still move me deeply or bring up a smile, maybe because, as Donald Richie said in his ground-breaking book on Ozu, this director shows us so much but tells us so little, and so we have to contribute a part of ourselves while watching.[1] Our involvement is deeper, and so is our experience. According to Kometani

1. Richie, *Ozu*, 109.

Shinnosuke, "Ozu's films are addictive because they offer a distinctive and appealing style that is specific only to Ozu."[2] Not being an expert film scholar myself, in an attempt to decipher that unique style, I've been returning time and again to David Bordwell's incomparable book on the poetics of Ozu's cinema, which is still an indispensable source for understanding the wider sphere in which Ozu created his films, as well as the rhyme and reason behind every shot.[3] The current short guide is in no way a substitute for these and other important books, but it has a few unique features which could assist those who come under the spell of Ozu's films, and need some information and guidance.

Ozu's films are beautiful to look at, even though their beauty has gradually faded, especially in the older films (some have been digitally restored). They are like other works of art—especially old films, but also paintings and other art objects—which are damaged, but their original beauty can still be discerned through the veils of time. The films' beauty is not lost even despite the unavoidable repeated watching on home media—for which these films were not created—since theatre screenings are rare.

Ozu's humanism and his respect for all the people in his films are evident—to give one example—through his famous craft: most of the time, the camera looks at the characters straight on, every person who speaks is seen in their natural size. The camera doesn't reduce them to insignificance, neither does it make giants out of them, even though it often looks at them from a slightly upward-looking angle, below eye level. We hardly ever see them from above, and when in a rare moment we do—such as the old couple facing the sea in *Tokyo Story*—the effect is breathtaking. Nor do we see the protagonists in extreme closeup, which invades their privacy. We view them as people like us, who, in most cases, lead their very normal lives. Sometimes they might be quite different from us socially, occasionally they are even ridiculed, but we can always understand them, feel what they are feeling and accept even their weaknesses.

2. Kometani, *Chasing Ozu*, 26.

3. Bordwell, *Ozu and the Poetics of Cinema.*

The stories in the films are often repeated, and the same actors appear again and again, often playing similar characters and called by similar names. This familiarity draws us in, into their assumed lives, making us almost a part of Ozu's large "family." Although it was somewhat accidental—the studio having insisted that Ozu in most cases use its own actors rather than hire from outside—I find it to be one of the most appealing characteristics of Ozu's films. Of course, it was not entirely accidental; Ozu intentionally used the same actors again and again to create certain characters, or allowed them to develop and mature in various ways. In fact, it was mainly the wish to identify these characters that led me to start the current work. Identifying the various and numerous actors and tracking their history proved to be a very time-consuming but enjoyable labor. Although such a list can never be exhaustive, I have tried to make it as comprehensive as possible, listing nearly 400 names of actors and actresses who appeared in Ozu's films.

The following chapter offers some basic biographical data on Ozu's life and work. This is followed by the main part of the book, listing in chronological order all the films directed by Ozu, many of which are lost. Besides the concise synopsis of the plots and some other details, for the surviving films I've added some personal observations, and for many of them also a short essay, usually focusing on one aspect of the film in question. As for the cast, an effort has been made to include the names of as many actors as possible for each film, both surviving and lost, based on opening credits, printed scripts, and various other sources. Since this book is directed at viewers (rather than experts), including those viewers who might have little or no experience of Japan, I have specified the roles played by each actor, often adding various details that will help identify them on the screen. Since they cannot be watched, I did not specify the characters portrayed in the films that were lost, only listed the names of the actors who are known to have been in them. Also included are a short personal epilog on watching Ozu's films, profiles of selected actors, a list of actors' names in alphabetical order with Japanese script and the films they appeared in, a table of Ozu's films, and an annotated bibliography.

This book has been many years in the making, as I was painstakingly combing many visual and printed sources, gradually accumulating all the details offered here about each film and actor. I wish to indicate that in writing it, no use was made either of AI or of translation software.

D.B.C.

Kyoto
March 2026

Biographical Sketch

OZU YASUJIRŌ WAS BORN on the 12th of December 1903 in Fukugawa, which was part of the "lower city" of Tokyo. His father was the manager of a family fertilizer business going back for several generations, mainly in Ise. His mother was from a merchant family, and he had an older and a younger brother, and two younger sisters. When he was nine years old the father sent his wife and children to his home town of Matsusaka in Mie Prefecture (western Honshu). Ozu was enrolled in a high school as a boarder, but was expelled due to discipline infringements, and later had to commute from home. He became fascinated with movies, especially American ones, and aspired to become a film director. In March 1921 he graduated from high school, but twice failed entrance exams to university, perhaps intentionally, and for about a year worked as a substitute teacher in the countryside. He finally returned to Tokyo with the rest of the family in March 1923.

In August 1923, with his uncle working as an intermediary, he was hired by the Shōchiku Film Company as an assistant in the cinematography department at their Kamata Studio. This was against the wishes of his father, who still hoped to have him continue in the family business. In December he was conscripted into the army, served for one year, and was discharged after reaching the rank of corporal. On returning to Shōchiku he was employed as an assistant director, and in 1927 was given the chance to direct his first film, *Sword of Penitence*, his only *jidai geki* (period film).

Ozu wrote the script for the film with Noda Kōgo, who would become his close collaborator for much of his career. Ozu then directed a string of light comedies, but gradually was allowed to make more substantial films, using Shōchiku's established stars. Between 1927 and 1937, Ozu directed thirty-six films, twenty-one of which are completely or mostly lost. The pace was not unusual, as the studios in Japan, like those in America and Europe, were producing films at a relentless pace; nor is the fact that many of the films were not preserved, after completing their runs at the cinema halls. His films of the 1920's and 30's depicted a wide range of social realities: the lives and aspirations of college students (including their romantic escapades), the struggles of lower-class office workers and their families, marital problems among lower and upper-middle class couples, as well as a few films about gangsters and "bad" ladies. During these years Ozu was experimenting with various genres and cinematic technics, gradually creating his own unique style of film making. Among his outstanding surviving films of the early to mid-1930's are *Tokyo Chorus, I Was Born, But . . . , Where Now Are the Dreams of Youth?, Dragnet Girl, Passing Fancy, Story of Floating Weeds, An Inn in Tokyo*, and a few others. Ozu began using sound later than other directors, as he had promised his photographer to wait for the sound system the latter was developing rather than use the one already installed by the studio. His first film with full sound and dialogue was *The Only Son* of 1936.

In September 1937, Ozu was called up for army reserve duty and dispatched to China, where Japan was waging a long and brutal war. He served on various fronts and saw battle several times, reaching the rank of sergeant. He was discharged from military service in July 1939. Surprisingly, the war experience did not seem to have any significant effect on his work, although memories of that period would appear in the post-war films.

During the following war years Ozu was able to direct only two films, which reflected the spirit and concerns of the times in some subtle ways, without displaying any overt militarism. These were *The Brothers and Sisters of the Toda Family* and *There was a Father*.

In 1943, Ozu was drafted into the army once again, this time for the purpose of making a documentary film about Japan's war in Burma, but was eventually sent to Singapore, where he had little to do. While there he was able to watch many pre-war American films that were not screened in Japan, including *Citizen Kane*, *Rebecca*, and many others. However, although he appreciated those films, they no longer affected his previously established style in any way. At the end of the war he was detained as a civilian, and spent about six months in a British detention camp. When Japanese citizens began to be repatriated, he gave up his place in favor of someone with a family. Ozu finally returned to Japan in February 1946, and immediately started working. His first two films reflected some aspects of the harsh reality of post-war Japan, while also constituting a continuation of his pre-war films. These were *Record of a Tenement Gentleman* and *A Hen in the Wind*.

Ozu resumed his collaboration with Noda Kōgo in 1948, and the two of them together wrote the scripts for the following thirteen Ozu films, which include many of his most memorable masterpieces, beginning with *Late Spring*, and followed by *Early Summer*, *Tokyo Story*, and others. As with the use of sound, Ozu resisted the introduction of color for a long while, directing his first color film, *Equinox Flower*, in 1958. This was followed by five more color films, all sublimely beautiful in different ways.

It is intriguing that Ozu, who grew up almost fatherless, who never married, and who had no children of his own, created so many sensitive films about fathers, about marital life, and parent-child relationships. He lived with his mother, who spoiled and loved him deeply until her death, a year before his own. Ozu was described as shy towards women, and although he was known to have had several affairs, these never led to cohabitation or marriage.

Ozu, who was a heavy drinker and smoker all his life, contracted a severe form of throat cancer. At first he was able to regard it with humor, but he had to endure great suffering during the final months of his life. He died on his sixtieth birthday and his ashes were buried in Engaku-ji, a Buddhist temple located in Kamakura near Tokyo, where he had lived with his mother since 1951.

Ozu's Films, Surviving and Lost

Apart from the fifty-three films listed below numerically, Ozu also made a short documentary film (see below under 1935), which brings up the number of his films to fifty-four on some lists. Twenty-one of his films were fully or partially lost, but the scripts survived for most of them, and in a few cases a digest or some media reports preserve the main plot and some other details. Of the thirty-two fully surviving films, twelve are silent and one has partial sound (1929-1935). Ozu was also late using color, which he did only in his six final films (1958-1962).

Ozu made almost all his films for his employer, the Shōchiku Film Company, except for three films for which he was loaned out to different studios at their request (below numbers 42, 50, and 52). In these cases he used cinematographers and on-set crew members different from his usual ones, as well as some different actors.

Ozu co-wrote most of his scripts. In the pre-war period he sometimes used pseudonyms for stories or scripts, most often "James Maki." Ikeda Tadao was a constant collaborator, involved in writing the script for sixteen of Ozu's films. Fushimi Akira was another constant collaborator. However, Ozu's most crucial collaborator in script writing was Noda Kōgo, with whom he wrote the script for his very first film. Noda also wrote the script for twelve of Ozu's silent movies, and starting from 1948, he and Ozu together wrote the scripts for all of the subsequent thirteen films.

The cinematographer in the pre-war years was often the editor too (in most cases it was Mohara Hideo), but in fact Ozu had full control of editing, which in a sense was already decided when the script was written. Most of Ozu's films since 1941 were shot by Atsuta Yūharu, who was previously Mohara's assistant, and the role of the editor was separate.

Beginning in 1924, the major Japanese film magazine *Kinema Jumpo* awarded their Best Ten Lists of the year, considered iconic and prestigious. An Ozu film first appeared on the list in 1930; this and the subsequent mentions are also indicated below for the relevant films. Ozu's films won twenty-three mentions on the top-ten list, including six first places, the last being *Early Summer*. His later films, which are so widely appreciated, won second place (*Tokyo Story*) or less, or no mention at all.

Beginning in 1949, Ozu's scripts indicate the age of the main characters (and also some minor ones), and this information is quoted below next to character's description in the cast lists of the relevant films. In most cases, one year should be deducted, because according to Japanese custom, babies are one year old at birth. This is particularly significant when considering the age of children or of women in their twenties who are expected to get married.

1927

1. B&W, Silent, Lost

Sword of Penitence

懺悔の刃　*Zange no yaiba*

Shōchiku Kamata Studio

Story by Ozu, script by Noda Kōgo

Cinematography: Aoki Isamu

No script, negative or prints survive

Ozu's only *jidai geki* (period film). The plot is about two criminal brothers trying to reform but failing. Two women try to save them, but one of them is killed.

Cast:

Azuma Saburō, Ogawa Kunimatsu, Kawara Kanji, Nodera Shōichi, Atsumi Eiko, Hanayagi Miyako, Konami Hatsuko, Kawamura Reikichi

1928

2. B&W, Silent, Lost

The Dreams of Youth

若人の夢 *Wakōdo no yume*

Shōchiku Kamata Studio

Story and script by Ozu

Cinematography: Mohara Hideo

No script, negative or prints survive

A comedy about college dormitory life, involving mainly two students and their girlfriends.

Cast:

Saitō Tatsuo, Wakaba Nobuko, Yoshitani Hisao, Matsui Junko, Sakamoto Takeshi, Ōyama Kenji, Takamatsu Eiko, Seki Tokio, Ogura Shigeru

*

3. B&W, Silent, Lost

Wife Lost

女房紛失　*Nyōbō funshitsu*

Shōchiku Kamata Studio

Story by Takano Ononosuke, script by Yoshida Momosuke

Cinematography: Mohara Hideo

No script, negative or prints survive

A light comedy concerning a marital mix-up, involving a young couple, a dancer, and a detective.

Cast:

Saitō Tatsuo, Okamura Ayako, Okajima Shōichi, Sugano Shichirō, Sakamoto Takeshi, Seki Tokio, Matsui Junko, Ogura Shigeru

*

4. B&W, Silent, Lost

Pumpkin

カボチャ　*Kabocha*

Shōchiku Kamata Studio

Story by Ozu, script by Kitamura Komatsu

Cinematography: Mohara Hideo

No script, negative or prints survive

A short comedy about a young man and his misadventures with several girlfriends.

Cast:

Saitō Tatsuo, Hinatsu Yurie, Handa Hidemaru, Kozakura Yōko, Sakamoto Takeshi

*

5. B&W, Silent, Lost

A Couple on the Move

引越し夫婦 *Hikkoshi fūfu*

Shōchiku Kamata Studio

Story by Kikuchi Ippei, script by Fushimi Akira

Cinematography: Mohara Hideo

Script exists, but no negative or prints

A comedy about a young couple moving from house to house and involved in various misunderstandings.

Cast:

Watanabe Atsushi, Yoshikawa Mitsuko, Ōkuni Ichirō, Nakahama Ichizō, Naniwa Tomoko, Ōyama Kenji

*

6. B&W, Silent, Lost

Body Beautiful

肉体美 *Nikutaibi*

Shōchiku Kamata Studio

Story and script by Fushimi Akira

Cinematography: Mohara Hideo

Script exists, but no negative or prints

A comedy, which was also considered a home drama (Ozu's first), about a young couple who pose as each other's artist's model, and reconcile after some marital trouble.

Cast:

Saitō Tatsuo, Iida Chōko, Kimura Kenji, Ōyama Kenji, Sakamoto Takeshi, Himori Shinichi

1929

7. B&W, Silent, Lost

Treasure Mountain

宝の山　*Takara no yama*

Shōchiku Kamata Studio

Story by Ozu, script by Fushimi Akira

Cinematography: Mohara Hideo

Script exists, but no negative or prints

A comedy about a young man falling in love with a geisha.

Cast:

Kobayashi Tokuji, Hinatsu Yurie, Aoyama Mariko, Okamura Ayako, Iida Chōko, Naniwa Tomoko, Wakami Takiko, Itokawa Kyōko

*

8. B&W, Silent

Days of Youth

若き日　*Wakaki hi*

Known also by a longer title:

学生ロマンス 若き日　*Gakusei romansu wakaki hi*

("A Students' Romance: Days of Youth")

Shōchiku Kamata Studio

Story and script by Fushimi Akira, with revisions by Ozu

Cinematography: Mohara Hideo

Running time: 103 minutes

The First Survivor

Ozu's earliest surviving film is a comedy involving two students, Watanabe and Yamamoto, who compete for the love of a girl, Chieko. After finishing their exams, the two join a college ski club for a holiday in the mountains, where they unexpectedly encounter Chieko. They court her but discover she is there for an arranged-marriage meeting with Hatamoto, the head of the ski club. Disappointed, they take the train back to Tokyo, only to encounter a professor who reports their failing grades. Watanabe then promises to find Yamamoto a girlfriend by using the same trick he used to get to know Chieko at the beginning of the film. Although slight in comparison with his later films, it is clear from watching this one that Ozu has already mastered his trade.

Cast:

The opening credits list fifteen names of actors, matched with their roles.

Watanabe Bin, a student—Yūki Ichirō
Yamamoto Shuichi, a student—Saitō Tatsuo
Chieko—Matsui Junko
Chieko's aunt—Iida Chōko
Boarding house landlady—Takamatsu Eiko
Her son Katsuji—Kofujita Shōichi
Professor Anayama—Ōkuni Ichirō
Professor—Sakamoto Takeshi
Hatamoto, a student and head of the ski club—Himori Shinichi
Kobayashi, a student—Yamada Fusao
Students:
Ryū Chishū
Ogura Shigeru
Ichiki Toppa
Nishikori Bin
Hachino Toyoo

*

9. B&W, Silent, Mostly lost
Fighting Friends—Japanese Style
和製喧嘩友達 *Wasei kenka tomodachi*

Shōchiku Kamata Studio
Story and script by Noda Kōgo
Cinematography: Mohara Hideo
Script exists, but no negative or prints; fourteen out of seventy-seven minutes were restored from amateur-format 9.5 mm film.

A comedy about two truck-driving friends who start quarreling after falling in love with the same girl, who eventually marries someone else. The two later repair their friendship, driving their truck alongside the train that is taking the newlyweds on their honeymoon, all waving happily to each other. Only the first and last few minutes of the film survive (restored footage is available on the Internet).

Cast:

Watanabe Atsushi, Yoshitani Hisao, Takamatsu Eiko, Yūki Ichirō, Ōkuni Ichirō, Naniwa Tomoko, Wakaba Nobuko

*

10. B&W, Silent, Mostly lost

I Graduated, But . . .

大学は出たけれど *Daigaku wa detakeredo*

Shōchiku Kamata Studio

Story and script by Shimizu Hiroshi and Aramaki Yoshio

Cinematography: Mohara Hideo

Script exists, but no negative or prints; ten out of seventy minutes were restored from amateur-format 9.5 mm film.

A college graduate refuses a job offer that seems beneath him, but has to pretend he is employed for the sake of his mother and fiancée. After getting married the wife learns the truth, and starts working in a bar. They fight and reconcile, and on returning for the job he rejected, he is offered a better one. This film was a certain turning point for Ozu, from light comedies to the harsh realities of unemployed graduates and the life of office workers. The surviving scenes offer a digest of the main storyline (restored footage is available on the Internet).

Cast:

Takada Minoru, Tanaka Kinuyo, Suzuki Utako, Ōyama Kenji, Kimura Kenji, Sakamoto Takeshi, Himori Shinichi, Iida Chōko, Ryū Chishū, Kofujita Shōichi, Mōri Teruo

*

11. B&W, Silent, Lost

The Life of an Office Worker

会社員生活 *Kaishain seikatsu*

Shōchiku Kamata Studio

Story by Ozu, script by Noda Kōgo

Cinematography: Mohara Hideo

No script, negative or prints in existence

A couple are eagerly expecting the husband's end-of-year bonus, but in fact he was fired and has difficulty finding another job, which causes marital friction. Eventually a friend helps him find a new job.

Cast:

Saitō Tatsuo, Yoshikawa Mitsuko, Kofujita Shōichi, Katō Seiichi, Aoki Tomio, Sakamoto Takeshi

*

12. B&W, Silent, Mostly lost

A Straightforward Boy

突貫小僧 *Tokkan kozō* (Literally: "A boy who charges into you")

Shōchiku Kamata Studio

Story by "Nozu Chuji," script by Ikeda Tadao

Cinematography: Nomura Ko

Script exists, but no negative or prints; eighteen out of thirty-seven minutes were restored from amateur-format 9.5 mm film.

A short film about a boy being kidnapped but driving his kidnappers mad with his demands for sweets and toys until they give up and release him. Surviving scenes are from the beginning and end of the film (restored footage is available on the Internet). The child actor Aoki Tomio became so famous that he adopted the film's title as his screen name, and was to have major roles in several Ozu films of the 1930's.

Cast:

Saitō Tatsuo, Sakamoto Takeshi, Aoki Tomio

1930

13. B&W, Silent, Lost

An Introduction to Marriage

結婚学入門　*Kekkongaku nyūmon*

Shōchiku Kamata Studio

Story by Okuma Toshio, script by Noda Kōgo

Cinematography: Mohara Hideo

Script exists, but no negative or prints

A husband and a wife are tired of each other and get involved in the life of another troubled couple. A comedy in the tradition of Ernst Lubitsch, involving the urban upper middle class.

Cast:

Saitō Tatsuo, Kurishima Sumiko, Nara Shinyō, Okamura Fumiko, Takada Minoru, Tatsuta Shizue, Yoshikawa Mitsuko

*

14. B&W, Silent

Walk Cheerfully

朗かに歩め *Hogarakani ayume*

Shōchiku Kamata Studio

Story by Shimizu Hiroshi, script by Ikeda Tadao

Cinematography: Mohara Hideo

Running time: 96 minutes

Ozu's Take on Hollywood Gangsters

Those viewers familiar only with Ozu's post-war films will be greatly surprised on watching this one but will also recognize Ozu's evolving style. This "gangster" movie, heavily influenced in its subject matter and somewhat in its style by contemporary American films, but with a clear Japanese twist, opens with a long sequence in which the camera is moving like in no other Ozu film. A petty thief, Senko, is being pursued by a mob, but manages to prove his innocence. The story then focuses on his brother Kenji, a young but stylish delinquent, as he starts caring for an innocent girl, Yasue, who is trying to avoid the advances of her boss, Ono. Kenji has a *moga* (the Japanese condensed phrase for the "modern girls" who broke with the traditional appearances and behavior expected of young women) girlfriend, Chieko, who happens to work for Ono's company, and helps him lure Yasue to a hotel, but Kenji is there to save her. The brothers decide to go straight, so Senko gets a job as a chauffeur for a hotel and arranges for Kenji to work as a window cleaner. Their old accomplices

Gunpei and Chieko try to convince the brothers to help in their next crime and are rejected, but when these two are caught by the police, they divulge Kenji's past misdemeanors. The brothers are arrested and spend several months in jail but are happily reunited with Yasue and her family in the end.

Cast:

The opening credits list the names of eight actors and their roles. Some uncredited actors were identified, and descriptions of characters added.

Koyama Kenji, a young delinquent—Takada Minoru
Senko, Kenji's brother—Yoshitani Hisao
Sugimoto Yasue, an innocent girl—Kawasaki Hiroko
    Her younger sister, Mitsuko—Matsuzono Nobuko
    Her mother—Suzuki Utako
Chieko, Kenji's *moga* girlfriend—Date Satoko
Gunpei, Chieko's accomplice—Mōri Teruo
Ono, the company manager—Sakamoto Takeshi

Uncredited:
The hotel manager—Kimura Kenji
Detective—Kawara Kanji
Man in a billiard parlor—Saitō Tatsuo

*

15. B&W, Silent
I Flunked, But . . .
落第はしたけれど *Rakudai wa shita keredo*

Shōchiku Kamata Studio
Story by Ozu, script by Fushimi Akira
Cinematography: Mohara Hideo
Running time: 64 minutes

The Unfulfilled Promise of Higher Education

This film is a short comedy about college life. The student Takahashi lives in a rented apartment with four student friends and is liked by the girl working at the café next door. However, he has another set of four friends who constantly try to cheat in the exams. Takahashi copies the exam material on the back of his shirt, but his plan fails as his landlady sends the shirt to be washed. While his roommates graduate, Takahashi and his other four friends fail. However, the graduates are idle, unable to secure jobs, while Takahashi and his friends return happily to school and become cheerleaders.

Although this film is not one of Ozu's outstanding works to survive from this period, it is often very funny, and includes many scenes of acting in unison, which Ozu will use more subtly in his later films. It is also an opportunity to see the very young and charming Tanaka Kinuyo (seen here folding the clothes her boyfriend is taking off, just as she does with her husband's nearly three decades later in *Equinox Flower*), and also the young Ryū Chishū in a first substantial—albeit minor—role (according to him, after participating in all of Ozu's previous films in small, uncredited roles, it was the first time he was given a copy of the script). The problem of college graduates failing to secure the kind of decent jobs they could have expected is repeated in several Ozu films of the 1930's.

Cast:
The opening credits list the names of fourteen actors and their roles.

Takahashi, a student—Saitō Tatsuo

Okane, the landlady—Futaba Kaoru

Her son, Ginbō—Aoki Tomio

First professor—Wakabayashi Hiroo

Second professor—Ōkuni Ichirō

Café girl, Sayoko—Tanaka Kinuyo

Failed students:

Ōmura—Yokoo Dekao

Koike—Seki Tokio

Ishikawa—Mikura Hiroshi

Cheer team—Yokoyama Gorō

Successful students:

Sugimoto—Tsukita Ichirō

Hattori—Ryū Chishū

Yokoyama—Yamada Fusao

Suzuki—Satomi Kenji

*

16. B&W, Silent

That Night's Wife

その夜の妻　*Sono yo no tsuma*

Shōchiku Kamata Studio

Story by Oscar Shisgall, "From Nine to Nine," script by Noda Kōgo

Cinematography: Mohara Hideo

Running time: 65 minutes

Playing Cops and Robbers

The film opens with a night scene featuring the police, and an office where people have been tied and gaged by an armed robber. It turns out that the robber is an artist who committed the crime in order to save his critically ill daughter. Evading the police he returns home in a taxi but is followed into the apartment by the taxi driver, who is in fact a police detective. The wife uses her husband's handgun to stop the detective from arresting him, but as the night drags on she falls asleep and the detective turns the tables on her. The husband had vowed to turn himself in if the child survives the night, but the detective, seeing his dedication to his daughter, is willing to look the other way and let him escape. He leaves, but soon comes back, giving himself up rather than facing a life on the run. The film combines the contemporary genres of crime thriller and family melodrama, but is executed in Ozu's characteristic style, with some flashes of his familiar humor.

Cast:

The opening credits list the names of five actors and their roles. One more uncredited actor was identified.

The husband, Hashizume Shuji—Okada Tokihiko

His wife, Mayumi—Yagumo Emiko

Their daughter, Michiko—Ichimura Mitsuko

Kagawa, police detective—Yamamoto Tōgō

Doctor Sugita—Saitō Tatsuo

Uncredited:

Policeman—Ryū Chishū

*

17. B&W, Silent, Lost
The Revengeful Spirit of Eros
エロ神の怨霊　*Erogami no onryō*

Shōchiku Kamata Studio
Story by Ishihara Seizaburō, script by Noda Kōgo
Cinematography: Mohara Hideo
No script, negative or prints in existence

A couple is trying to commit a lovers' suicide by jumping into the sea, but both survive the attempt and become hostile to each other. This film, which he made in a few days during a vacation at a spa, is reputed to have been Ozu's most insignificant one.

Cast:
Saitō Tatsuo, Hoshi Hikaru, Date Satoko, Tsukida Ichirō

*

18. B&W, Silent, Lost
Lost Luck
足に触った幸運　*Ashi ni sawatta kōun*　(Literally: "The luck which touched the leg")

Shōchiku Kamata Studio
Story and script by Noda Kōgo
Cinematography: Mohara Hideo
Script exists, but no negative or prints

A man is rewarded for returning money that somebody had lost, but this only brings him trouble at work and with his wife. Contemporary reviews found the film to be a mix of humor and melancholy.

Cast:

Saitō Tatsuo, Yoshikawa Mitsuko, Aoki Tomio, Ichimura Mitsuko, Sakamoto Takeshi, Mōri Teruo, Tsukita Ichirō, Seki Tokio, Ōkuni Ichirō

*

19. B&W, Silent, Lost

Young Miss

お嬢さん *Ojōsan*

Shōchiku Kamata Studio

Story by Kitamura Komatsu, Gags by Fushimi Akira, "James Maki," and Ikeda Tadao

Cinematography: Mohara Hideo

Script exists, but no negative or prints

A tie for second place in the contemporary-life division of *Kinema Jumpo* list (a first for Ozu)

An episodic comedy involving two male reporters and one female who beats them to scoops. The film had a high production value, was a commercial and critical success, and won Ozu his first mention on the *Kinema Jumpo* yearly list of best films.

Cast:

Kurishima Sumiko, Okada Tokihiko, Saitō Tatsuo, Tanaka Kinuyo, Ōkuni Ichirō, Yamamoto Tōgō, Okada Sōtarō, Ogura Shigeru, Tatsuta Shizue, Mōri Teruo, Naniwa Tomoko, Yokoo Dekao, Hikari Kimiko

1931

20. B&W, Silent

The Lady and the Beard

淑女と髭　*Shukujo to hige*

Shōchiku Kamata Studio

Story and script by Kitamura Komatsu, Gags by "James Maki"

Cinematography: Mohara Hideo

Shot in January 1931

Running time: 75 minutes

Shave the Beard and Win the Girl

This film is a light comedy with a large cast, often quite funny, and ending on a degree of pathos. It opens with a farcical *kendo* match between the teams of two universities (the head referee is a young boy, Ozu's regular at the time). The winner is the thickly bearded Okajima, and he is invited by his friend Teruo to go to his home on the occasion of his sister's birthday. On his way there Okajima rescues an innocent girl, Hiroko, who is being robbed by a rough girl, Sayoko, and he also beats up her two accomplices who appear on the scene. His friend's family turns out to be very rich and snobbish (to a degree probably not yet seen in an Ozu film), and he is rejected by the sister Ikuko and her girlfriends as too traditional and boring. Later Hiroko, the girl he saved, advises Okajima to shave off his beard in order to secure a job. They become engaged with the help of her mother, and he finds work in a travel agency situated in a hotel. The gang had been following him, and Sayoko tries to involve him in stealing a brooch (which was given to a weeping lady by a foreigner, probably a German, a rare appearance by a non-Japanese in an Ozu film), but he thwarts her plan and later takes her to his room to watch over her. The snobbish Ikuko, who meanwhile rejected a rich suitor for the beardless Okajima, appears on the scene with her mother and brother, but they retreat on seeing another woman there. However, when Hiroko arrives in the morning, she shows that she trusts her fiancé. Sayoko leaves, promising to start a new life.

Cast:

The opening credits list the names of twelve actors and their roles. One uncredited actor was identified, and some descriptions of roles added.

Okajima Kiichi, "the beard"—Okada Tokihiko

Hiroko, the innocent girl, works as a typist—Kawasaki Hiroko

Her mother—Iida Chōko

Moga ("modern girl"), Satoko—Date Satoko

Okajima's friend Yukimoto Teruo, son of the baron —Tsukida Ichirō

Ikuko, his sister—Iizuka Toshiko

Their mother—Yoshikawa Mitsuko

Their butler—Sakamoto Takeshi

Company manager—Okada Sōtarō

A rich *mobo* ("modern boy"), rejected by Ikuko—Nanjo Yasuo

His mother—Katsuragi Fumiko

Head of the opposing kendo team—Saitō Tatsuo

Uncredited:

Kendo head referee—Aoki Tomio

*

21. B&W, Silent, Lost

Beauty's Sorrows

美人哀愁 *Bijin aishū*

Shōchiku Kamata Studio

Story by Henri de Regnier, Adaptation by "James Maki," Script by Ikeda Tadao

Cinematography: Mohara Hideo

Script exists, but no negative or prints

A romantic melodrama involving a woman and two men, one who has the sculpture for which the woman modeled, and the other who marries her. By the end of the long film, all three are dead and the sculpture is smashed. The film was a critical failure and Ozu avoided such material for the rest of his career.

Cast:

Okada Tokihiko, Saitō Tatsuo, Inoue Yukiko, Okada Sōtarō, Yoshikawa Mitsuko, Wakamizu Teruko, Nara Shinyō, Iizuka Toshiko

*

22. B&W, Silent

Tokyo Chorus

東京の合唱 *Tōkyō no gasshō*

Title at the background of opening credits: *Le chorus de Tokio*

Shōchiku Kamata Studio
Script by Noda Kōgo
Cinematography: Mohara Hideo
Running time: 90 minutes
Number three on the *Kinema Jumpo* list

Old and Flickering

Can people today really enjoy old, flickering, black & white, silent movies? Even in my childhood, which was a long time ago, such films—those of Charlie Chaplin, Laurel & Hardy etc.—seemed strange, almost as if coming from another world. Since then, the experience of watching films has turned several times over, and most people nowadays are only accustomed to watching things that are colorful, noisy and fast. So, are these old films only viewed, if at all, by students of cinema who are made to watch them, by some dedicated cynophiles, or, in this case, those enthusiasts who feel they must watch every surviving film by Ozu, no matter what? I can't really tell, but I can say that watching these films is rewarding in various ways, as I mentioned when describing the earlier surviving ones. In the case of this film, Ozu's sixth to survive, I can honestly say that it is often very funny, that at the same time it is also poignant and touching, and that Ozu is already at the top of his game.

We first see the protagonist Okajima in high school, cheekily confronting a disciplinarian teacher. The story then jumps forward to his life as a married office worker with three young children. However, he hasn't changed, and is not afraid to challenge authority. When an elderly colleague is unfairly fired, he confronts the company's manager, and for his efforts gets fired too. The family falls on hard times: being college educated, he is over-qualified for the jobs on offer. Then, his daughter falls ill, and the hospital bills run high. He happens to meet his old schoolteacher who now owns a restaurant, and who offers him a part-time job advertising his business on the streets of Tokyo. Okajima agrees reluctantly, as the teacher promises to help him find a better job later on. His wife is disappointed in him, but eventually acquiesces. During a class reunion at the restaurant he is informed that a school job has transpired, but it is very long way from Tokyo. Relief is mixed with sadness for the couple, and even for the teacher.

Two scenes remained vividly with me since I first watched this film decades ago. One is when the wife comes back from the hospital with the recovered daughter. Her husband immediately engages the children in a merry clapping game, but she is shocked when opening the cabinet drawers to find them empty, save for mothballs, her kimonos gone to pay the hospital bills. She half-recovers to join in the game, but we can see how shocked and hurt she is. Another is when the wife and children are riding a streetcar, suddenly seeing the father on the street carrying a poll with an advertisement for the restaurant. The wife says it couldn't be him (it simply couldn't!) but the children look at each other and confirm: "it was papa."

The part of the father is played by the wonderfully talented Okada Tokihiko, who stared in several of Ozu's silent films and was a close friend, but tragically died at the age of thirty from tuberculosis. He left behind an infant daughter, Mariko, who grew up to star in two of Ozu's final films. Ozu's "family" was sometimes literally that.

There is a little mystery, however, about the identity of the girl who plays Okada's lively daughter in this film. All sources indicate that it was Takamine Hideko, who was born in April 1924, and seems to be the correct age of about seven. Takamine would grow to become one of Japan's most celebrated actresses, and two decades later would play the spirited younger sister in Ozu's *The Munakata Sisters*. However, various lists include this film on the résumé of another child actress of the time, Ichimura Mitsuko, who was the daughter in *That Night's Wife* the previous year. Looking at the two girls with their identical bobbed hair it is indeed difficult to tell them apart. However, Ichimura was born in May 1926, so was probably too young to portray the girl we see in *Tokyo Chorus*, and the inclusion of this film on her résumé is probably a mistake. Unlike Takamine's, Ichimura's acting career was short, ending in the early 1940's.

Cast:

The opening credits list the names of ten actors and their roles. Some uncredited actors were identified, and some descriptions of roles added.

Okajima Shinji, seen first as a student and then as a fired *salaryman*—Okada Tokihiko

His wife, Sugako—Yagumo Emiko

Their son—Sugawara Hideo

Their daughter, Miyoko—Takamine Hideko

The teacher, Ōmura—Saitō Tatsuo

Ōmura's wife—Iida Chōko

Elderly company employee, Yamada—Sakamoto Takeshi

Company president—Tani Reikō

His male secretary—Miyajima Kenichi

Boisterous company employee—Yamaguchi Isamu

Uncredited:

Doctor—Kawara Kanji

Former student at party—Ryū Chishū

1932

23. B&W, Silent, Lost

Spring Comes from the Ladies

春は御婦人から *Haru wa gofujin kara*

Shōchiku Kamata Studio

Story by "James Maki," Script by Ikeda Tadao

Cinematography: Mohara Hideo

Script exists, but no negative or prints

A comedy about college students, some romances, and a tailor who is unable to collect payments due to him.

Cast:

Shirota Jirō, Saitō Tatsuo, Inoue Yukiko, Izumi Hiroko, Sakamoto Takeshi, Tani Reikō

*

24. B&W, Silent

I Was Born, But . . .

生れてはみたけれど *Umarete wa mita keredo*

This film also has a pre-title:

大人の見る繪本 *Otona no miru ehon* "A Picture Book for Adults"

Shōchiku Kamata Studio

Story by "James Maki," Script by Fushimi Akira

Cinematography: Mohara Hideo

Running time: 90 minutes

Number one on the *Kinema Jumpo* list (Ozu's first at the top of the list)

The First Masterpiece?

By this point in his career Ozu had already made several memorable films, but various critics consider this one to be his first masterpiece. It is indeed a very impressive film, but personally I have certain reservations. As David Bordwell writes, this is "an unusually explicit demonstration of a lesson. Most Ozu films of whatever period have an elusiveness of connotation that *I Was Born, But . . .* almost wholly lacks. By means of its organizational unity and stylistic control, the film achieves great didactic rigor."[1] Perhaps too great.

I Was Born, But . . . is a comic film with a serious, perhaps even dark message, focusing on social power and weakness. It opens with a family of four moving to a suburb of Tokyo, and with shots of one wheel of the movers' truck stuck in the mud, perhaps an allegory of the father's life and prospects. This father, Mr. Yoshii, has moved his family in order to live closer to his boss, Iwasaki, with whom he is eager to curry favor. The family's two young sons get into trouble with a bully and skip school but are reported to the father by their teacher. With the help of an older boy they manage to deter the bully, and take over the boys' gang, which includes Iwasaki's son. Believing their father to be the best, the boys are disillusioned on seeing him in an amateur movie making a fool of himself for the sake of entertaining his boss. They have a big fight during which the father spanks the elder boy; the boys then go on a hunger strike, but the next day they reconcile. Between the two of them, the parents acknowledge that their children's future will probably be no better than theirs.

When watching this film I always felt that although it is no doubt comparable to Ozu's other films in style and subject matter, it is also somewhat different. For one thing, the pace seems relentless. Everything is focused on delivering the message, and there is hardly a moment to breathe free. Ozu's execution of each shot and sequence and the overall construction of the film are as brilliant as ever, but there are no "empty" shots or intermediate spaces

1. Bordwell, *Ozu and the Poetics of Cinema*, 224.

between scenes to which Ozu has already accustomed his viewers (these shots all seem to appear in the few minutes of Iwasaki's home movie which we share).

The children believe in raw power, not yet knowing that in the adult world power is social and has to do with position and money. They don't understand why their father has to bow down to his boss while they were able to subjugate his son and the rest of the kids. By the end of the film, they understand better. The lesson is a bitter one, but there is also a positive resolution in that the family comes together again.

Cast:

The opening credits list the names of sixteen actors and their roles. One uncredited actor was identified.

Yoshii Kennosuke, an office worker, the father—Saitō Tatsuo
His wife, Eiko—Yoshikawa Mitsuko
Their elder son, Ryōichi—Sugawara Hideo
Their younger son, Keiji—Tokkan Kozō
The boss, Iwasaki Sōhei—Sakamoto Takeshi
His wife—Hayami Teruyo
Their son, Tarō—Katō Seiichi
Saké store boy, Shinkō—Kofujita Shōichi
The teacher, Itō—Nishimura Seiji
The bully, Kamekichi—Iijima Zentarō
The children's playmates:
Fujimatsu Shōtarō
Hayama Masao
Satō Michio
Hayashi Kuniyasu
Nomura Akio
Ishiwatari Teruaki

Uncredited:

Subordinate running the projector—Ryū Chishū

*

25. B&W, Silent

Where Now Are the Dreams of Youth?

青春の夢いまいづこ *Seishun no yume ima izuko*

Shōchiku Kamata Studio

Story and script by Noda Kōgo

Cinematography: Mohara Hideo

Running time: 86 minutes

A Film of Two Parts

This film seems to be the combination of two parts, a comic one and a serious one, although the comic side can be said to have a serious, even brutal tone, and the serious part has some comic flashes. It is all executed masterfully through Ozu's sure and steady hand and the actors' performances.

The film opens like one of Ozu's typical college comedies, more or less where *I Flunked, But . . .* ended. The students are busy cheerleading and cheating in the exams. One of them, Tetsuo, comes from a rich family, and on returning home, drinks with his father. In a somewhat too long sequence, the father helps his son to get rid of a potential bride introduced to him by his uncle, and the comedy here becomes almost cruel. Later, while sitting an exam, Tetsuo is informed that his father is critically ill, and he rushes to his deathbed. He must now quit school and take his father's place as the company director. A year later, his three best friends come asking for jobs, and he gives them the answers to the company's entrance exam, as if they were all still in school. Tetsuo then renews his interest in Oshige, the girl who used to work in the western-style bakery-restaurant near the campus and decides to marry her. On telling his three friends of his intention, they express no reservations, although we can tell something is wrong. He then receives a visit from the mother of Saiki, one of the three, who comes to thank him for employing her son, and reveals by chance that he is engaged to Oshige. Visiting the girl, Tetsuo learns that she didn't believe that her feelings for him were reciprocated, and that she felt sorry for Saiki, who was the weakest in the group, and decided to support him. Full of rage, Tetsuo confronts his friends, loses his temper and slaps Saiki's face repeatedly. But in the final scene they are all reconciled, and Saiki and Oshige leave for their honeymoon.

Tetsuo's anger is not only due to the fact that he will be losing the girl he loves, but also, and perhaps mainly, because of Saiki's cowardice, as he was willing to give up his fiancé in order not to cross his employer, thus also breaking up their old friendship. But can they indeed remain friends when one is the boss and the others depend on him? In fact, the dire economic situation following the world-wide crisis of 1929 is apparent. For example, Oshige says that her uncle closed down the restaurant because students could no longer afford to go there. While still in college, Saiki tells Oshige he is trying harder than the others because he must support his mother. He therefore gives precedence to keeping his job over any personal feelings, but it seems that this is the very point that infuriates Tetsuo, perhaps unfairly, because he comes from a much more secure place.

Still, following the violent night scene, the film ends on a positive note. The final scene depicts the company's workers spending their noon break on the flat roof of the office building, indulging in various sporting activities. This kind of scene also appears thirty years later in Ozu's last film, *An Autumn Afternoon*. Furthermore, the three friends intend to wave goodbye to the newlyweds who are going on their honeymoon, as they pass by on the train. And indeed, they see the couple, who wave back at them. This scene is reflected decades later in *Late Autum*, albeit with a disappointing result: the friends on the roof—two girls in this case—are waving, but the couple on the train do not wave back.

In the role of Tetsuo, Egawa Ureo gives a very impressive performance, his first in an Ozu film. Saitō Tatsuo, one of Ozu's two most constant actors of the silent era, who played the father in *I Was Born, But . . .* , is here even more docile in the role of Saiki. Date Satoko is the cheeky *moga* rejected by Tetsuo. Tanaka Kinuyo and Ryū Chishū play roles similar to those they had in *I Flunked, But . . .* , although much more substantial ones in this case. Veteran Sakamoto Takeshi gives a brilliant comic performance as the college janitor and will play major roles as "Kihachi" in four Ozu films in the coming years.

This was Ozu's last student comedy, as well as his final *salaryman* film for a long time to come. In spite of the sometimes uneasy feeling of the film being made up of two different ingredients, it is masterly executed in every detail.

Cast:

The opening credits list the names of thirteen actors and their roles. They are listed below in a somewhat different order, with some descriptions of roles added.

Student, later company director Horino Tetsuo—Egawa Ureo

Tetsuo's father, Horino Kenzō, the former director —Takeda Shunrō

Their old housekeeper—Futaba Kaoru

Tetsuo's uncle, Kanzō, deputy director of the company —Mizushima Ryotarō

Bakery girl near the university, Oshige—Tanaka Kinuyo

College janitor—Sakamoto Takeshi

Students, later company employees:

Saiki Taichiō—Saitō Tatsuo

His mother—Iida Chōko

Kumada Junsuke—Ōyama Kenji

Shimazaki Shōgo—Ryū Chishū

Moga, Yuriko—Date Satoko

Her mother, Baroness Yamamura—Katsuragi Fumiko

Second candidate bride—Hanaoka Kikuko

*

26. B&W, Silent, Lost

Until the Day We Meet Again

また逢ふ日まで *Mata au hi made*

Shōchiku Kamata Studio

Script by Noda Kōgo

Cinematography: Mohara Hideo

Script exists, but no negative or prints

Number seven on the *Kinema Jumpo* list

A young man, having been disowned by his prosperous family for loving a prostitute, is drafted, and prepares to go to war without informing his father. However, the woman informs the family, and they hurry to the station as the train is pulling out. The woman goes back on the street.

Cast:

Okada Yoshiko, Oka Jōji, Nara Shinyō, Kawasaki Hiroko, Iida Chōko, Date Satoko, Yoshikawa Mitsuko

1933

27. B&W, Silent

Woman of Tokyo

東京の女 *Tōkyō no onna*

Shōchiku Kamata Studio

Story by Ernest Schwartz, Script by Noda Kōgo and Ikeda Tadao

Cinematography: Mohara Hideo

Running time: 47 minutes

A Tragedy of Misunderstanding

This short, somewhat atypically melodramatic film, is executed in what by now became Ozu's familiar style of filmmaking, including the low-angle camera, the short cuts, the transition shots, the elliptical narration (what is not shown on the screen but is made known to us in various indirect ways), and so on.

The plotline is straightforward and takes place over two days and a night. Ryōichi, a student, lives in a small apartment with his older sister Chikako, who works as a typist and pays for his tuition. A policeman visits the office where Chikako works, asking questions about her. Harue, Ryōichi's girlfriend, lives with her older brother, who is a policeman. She learns from him that Chicako, while saying she works in the evenings for a certain professor, in fact moonlights at a nightclub, and is suspected of worse (apparently unlicensed prostitution). Harue wants to talk with Chikako to warn her to change her ways but finds only Ryōichi at the apartment and tells him what she has heard. Meanwhile we see Chikako at a nightclub calling her brother to say she'll be late, and then entering a client's car. When she returns home, Ryōichi is furious and confronts and slaps her face, while she tries to tell him she only did it for him, to support his education. He leaves her and is seen wandering the streets. The next morning, Chikako visits Harue to ask if she has seen her brother, but Harue then recieves a phone call from her own brother telling her that Ryōichi committed suicide. We then see both women crying over his body, while reporters who were alerted to the site cynically dismiss the story as not newsworthy.

Cast:

The opening credits list the names of four actors and their roles. Some uncredited actors were identified.

Chikako—Okada Yoshiko

Her brother, Ryōichi—Egawa Ureo

Harue, Ryōichi's girlfriend—Tanaka Kinuyo

Her brother, Kinoshita, a policeman—Nara Shinyō

Uncredited:

Reporters:

Ryū Chishū

Ōyama Kenji

*

28. B&W, Silent

Dragnet Girl

非常線の女 *Hijōsen no onna*

Shōchiku Kamata Studio

Story by "James Maki," Script by Ikeda Tadao

Cinematography: Mohara Hideo

Running time: 100 minutes

The Invisible Kiss

This is the last of three consecutive films that revolve around "bad girls," and a few scenes in it even go back to the earlier "gangster" film, *Walk Cheerfully*. Similar to the preceding *Woman of Tokyo*, here too a young woman, Tokiko, works as a typist in a large firm, but leads a double life on the edge of the law. In Tokiko's case, she lives with Jōji, a former boxer and the leader of a small-time gang. A student and a fledgling boxer, Hiroshi, joins the gang, while sponging on his sister Kazuko, who works at a Victor records shop. Jōji becomes attracted to Kazuko and listens to records in her shop. When Tokiko learns about it, she goes to see Kazuko and threatens her with a gun, but soon finds that she actually likes her. Tokiko then expresses her wish that Jōji and herself reform, but he gets angry and throws her out. She goes to the home of her company boss, who has been pursuing her with expensive gifts, but suddenly changes her mind and returns to Jōji, who now agrees to go straight. However, just then Hiroshi comes to ask for money to replace what he has been stealing from the till in Kazuko's shop, and Jōji decides to pull one last robbery so Hiroshi can return the money and go straight. Tokiko assists Jōji in robbing her boss, and they give the money to Hiroshi. It then seems that Jōji has changed his mind about reforming, and when the police come to their apartment, he pulls Tokiko out through the window and tries to escape. She begs him to surrender, and when he refuses shoots him in the leg. They finally give themselves up to the police while embracing and telling each other that in two or three years they'll be out and will start a new life.

The film follows contemporary American models to such a degree that much of the action takes place in a boxing club, a billiard hall, and a night club, where in the background girls can be seen practicing the new craze of yo-yo. Ozu used various sites in Yokohama, the most Western-like town in Japan at the time, as locations for this film. It is indeed so "Western" that perhaps for the only time in an Ozu film people are seen walking into apartments with their shoes on, contrary to all Japanese norms. But it is also very typically Ozu, in his familiar style and in some new twists. Near the end of the scene in which Tokiko confronts Kazuko and, to her own surprise, gets to like her, they are seen standing at a certain distance from each other; Tokiko then steps forward but the camera goes down to show only the women's legs and feet as they touch; when the camera goes up again Tokiko is already leaving, and Kazuko is putting her hand to her cheek as if she had been slapped, although in fact we realize she had been kissed, but Ozu does not show us this kiss, or hardly any other kiss in all his previous and subsequent films, save for a few chaste examples much later. He must have been very shy indeed, but was also restricted by the Japanese film code of the time, which was extremely prudish. And after portraying the traditional, kimono-clad girl in several previous films, Tanaka Kinuyo here plays the *moga* ("modern girl"), wearing fashionable western dresses, smoking cigarettes, playing billiard, waving a handgun, and asserting herself bravely against her various male counterparts. There are also several new faces, including Oka Jōji and the two other young women.

Incidentally, in both films where a robbery takes place, here and in the earlier *That Night's Wife*, the robber only takes part of the available money, apparently only the sum he needs and no more. In the previous case it was the father who needed to buy medicine for his daughter (but never actually does), and here it is Jōji who needs the money for Hiroshi and intends to reform. In both cases the crime doesn't seem realistic.

Cast:

The opening credits list the names of twelve actors and their roles. Two uncredited actors were identified, and some descriptions of roles added.

Jōji, the gang boss, a former boxer—Oka Jōji

His girlfriend, Tokiko, works as a typist—Tanaka Kinuyo

Hiroshi, a student and a fledgling boxer who joins the gang —Mitsui Kōji

His sister, Kazuko, works in a record shop —Mizukubo Sumiko

Misako, the girlfriend of a gang member—Aizome Yumeko

Senkō, a member of the gang—Takayama Yoshirō

Misawa—Kaga Kōji

Okazaki, the company president's son—Nanjo Yasuo

His male secretary—Tani Reikō

Toa Boxing Club manager—Takemura Nobuo

Dancehall master—Kashima Shunsaku

Police officer—Nishimura Seiji

Uncredited:

Policemen:

Ryū Chishū

Nishimura Seiji

*

29. B&W, Silent

Passing Fancy

出来ごころ *Dekigokoro*

Shōchiku Kamata Studio

Story by "James Maki," Script by Ikeda Tadao

Cinematography: Sugimoto Shōjirō

Running time: 103 minutes

Number one on the *Kinema Jumpo* list (Ozu's second)

Enter Kihachi

After a long string of films featuring rumbustious college students, lowly office workers, snobbish members of the upper bourgeoise, and even some fashion-conscious gangsters, we are suddenly in a different world, that of the lowest strata of day laborers. *Passing Fancy* was the first of what Ozu would call his *Kihachi mono*, a string of four, almost consecutive films in which the working-class protagonist was called Kihachi, all roles played by the same actor.

The film opens with a *Naniwa-bushi* traditional comical performance in front of an appreciative audience, while an elaborate gag is developing around a small discarded money purse. It is summer and men and women alike scratch, wipe, and fan themselves incessantly. Kihachi, a day laborer, is raising his son Tomio who is in elementary school and whose mother is unaccounted for. His next-door neighbor and co-worker at a beer brewery is Jirō, an army veteran who is suspicious of young women. They are assisted by Otome, a middle-aged woman who runs a small restaurant nearby. A lonely girl, Harue, appears on the scene asking for help, and Kihachi encourages Otome to take her in. Kihachi is attracted to Harue, but gradually it becomes clear that she is interested in Jirō, who rebuffs her. Kihachi sinks into careless, drunken habits, and fights with his son, who has been bullied by his schoolmates. Wishing to encourage Tomio, Kihachi gives him some money to spend, but the boy over-indulges on sweets and requires medical treatment. Jirō asks the neighborhood barber for a loan to pay for the hospital bill while intending to go to work in Hokkaido to earn back the money, but Harue begs him to stay, and he unexpectedly reveals his feelings for her. Kihachi refuses to let Jirō go, and although the barber is willing to forgo the debt, he boards the boat ferrying workmen to Hokkaido in Jirō's place. However, realizing how he misses his son, he jumps off the boat and swims back ashore.

Perhaps the most memorable sequence in this delightful film takes place about mid-way, between Kihachi and his son. Tomio is being bullied by a group of kids saying his father is stupid. He charges at them waving his wooden *geta* sandals, but then retreats due to being outnumbered. He returns home crying, and inadvertently or not, destroys his father's plant. Coming home, Kihachi slaps his face. Tomio calls Kihachi a fool and a drunk, and in a fit of rage slaps his face again and again. The father absorbs the blows quietly, and when Tomio sits down to do his homework, he apologizes, asking him not to hate this pitiful dad. Father and son embrace, crying. In a different film, this could have felt too melodramatic, but in this film, in which the son is smarter and more mature than his father, the scene is just right.

After playing minor roles in half of Ozu's earlier films—some particularly memorable, such as the elderly employee being fired in *Tokyo Chorus*, and several others—Sakamoto Takeshi finally gets the leading role as Kihachi, a role which he repeats in several future films, although in each one his character is somewhat different. His son is also a veteran of sorts: although only ten years old when this one was made, he had already appeared in seven Ozu films, including *Tokkan Kozō*, a title which he adopted as his screen name, and as the younger son in *I Was Born, But . . .* Together they make for an unforgettable performance.

Cast:

The opening credits list the names of six actors and their roles. Several uncredited actors were identified, and some descriptions of roles added.

Kihachi—Sakamoto Takeshi

His son, Tomio—Tokkan Kozō

Harue—Fushimi Nobuko

Jirō—Obinata Den

Otome—Iida Chōko

Barber—Tani Reikō

Uncredited:

Teacher—Nishimura Seiji

Class leader boy—Katō Seiichi

Boy taunting Tomio—Sugawara Hideo

Doctor—Yamada Nagamasa

Beer brewery superior—Ishiyama Yūji

Man on boat—Ryū Chishū

1934

30. B&W, Silent, Partially lost
A Mother Should Be Loved
母を恋わずや *Haha o kowazu ya*

Shōchiku Kamata Studio

Story by "Komiya Sūtarō," adapted by Noda Kōgo, Script by Ikeda Tadao

Cinematography: Aoki Isamu

Script in existence, no negative, prints lack the first and last reels

Running time: 71 minutes, the first and last reels are missing

The missing beginning and end impair our ability to enjoy the film, which viewed from its surviving parts alone is not considered one of Ozu's most memorable achievements. The story is about the relationships between two half-brothers whose father died while they were in school, and the mother who raises the elder son, born to the father's first wife, as her own. However, on learning the truth about his origin while in university, the elder son becomes bitter and fights with his brother and stepmother, but eventually they reconcile.

Cast: Iwata Yukichi, Yoshikawa Mitsuko, Obinata Den, Katō Seiichi, Mitsui Kōji, Nomura Akio, Nara Shinyō, Aoki Shinobu, Mitsukawa Kyōko, Ryū Chishū, Aizome Yumeko, Matsui Junko, Iida Chōko

*

31. B&W, Silent
Story of Floating Weeds
浮草物語 *Ukigusa monogatari*

Shōchiku Kamata Studio

Story by "James Maki," Script by Ikeda Tadao

Cinematography: Mohara Hideo

Running time: 86 minutes

Number one on the *Kinema Jumpo* list (Ozu's third in three consecutive years)

Far from Tokyo

Almost for the first time in his career, Ozu leaves behind the urban atmosphere of Tokyo with its various sub-cultures that he enjoyed depicting, and makes a film that takes place entirely in the remote countryside. Its protagonist is a Kihachi, but a somewhat more sophisticated one than the day laborer Kihachi of *Passing Fancy*, being the head of a small troop of actors, although it is made clear that he is not well-educated, and that the entertainment offered by his troop is unsophisticated at best. The troop, combined of nine souls including a young boy and his father, arrives by night in a mountain village which they had last visited—apparently not in the same ensemble—four years earlier. It is soon revealed that in this village, Kihachi has a former lover (or wife), Otsune, who runs a rustic restaurant while raising her college-aged son, Shinkichi, who doesn't know that Kihachi is his father, calling him "Uncle." On learning this, Kihachi's current mistress and leading actress Otaka starts a quarrel, eventually bribing the younger actress Otoki to seduce Shinkichi, which she does, but then falls in love with him. Outraged, Kihachi beats up both actresses. Meanwhile subsequent days of rain reduce attendance, and the troop is bankrupted. Kihachi sells his props to a secondhand dealer and pays for the other troop members' tickets home, then goes to Otsune's place with the intention of staying over. However, when Shinkichi returns that night with Otoki, Kihachi starts beating her up again until he is restrained by the boy, who he also hits. Otsune then reveals Kihachi's true identity, and the fact that he's been paying for the boy's education, but Shinkichi says he wants nothing to do with such a father. By the time he comes round, Kihachi has already left, after asking Otsune to take care of Otoki. At the train station Kihachi runs into Otaka, and the two make up and decide to form a new troop.

The title likens the peripatetic actors to weeds floating downstream without purpose. Kihachi could have stayed in the village and raised his son, but by choosing a life of wandering, in fact had given him up, and his attempts to start anew or decide on his son's future are doomed to fail. This is fate, and there is nothing to do but accept it, as Kihachi does.

Together with the streets of Tokyo, also gone are the elaborate cartoons which always served as background to the opening credits, replaced now by rustic burlap, which becomes one of Ozu's trademarks from now on, given up only with his final film. Twenty-five years hence, Ozu will remake this film in color as *Floating Weeds*. The current film won the director his third consecutive first place on the *Kinema Jumpo* list, but the beautiful remake did not make the list at all. By the late fifties, the critics' taste has demonstrably changed.

Cast:

The opening credits list the names of sixteen actors and their roles. One uncredited actor was identified, and some descriptions of roles added.

Kihachi (Ichikawa Sahanji), head of a troop of actors —Sakamoto Takeshi

Otsune, a restaurant owner and long ago Kihachi's lover —Iida Chōko

Shinkichi, Otsune's son—Mitsui Kōji

Otaka, an actress and Kihachi's current mistress—Yagumo Emiko

Otoki, a young actress—Tsubōchi Yoshiko

Tomibo, a child actor—Tokkan Kozō

His father—Tani Reikō

Yoshi-chan, an actor—Nishimura Seiji

Mākō, an actor—Yamada Nagamasa

Troop member—Aono Kiyoshi

Troop member—Yui Munenobu

Theater proprietor, waiting for the troop at the station—Hira Yōkō

Station attendant—Wakamiya Mitsuru

Secondhand dealer—Kake Shusuke

Barber's wife—Aoyama Mariko

Villager—Ikebe Mitsumura

Uncredited:

Shouting audience member—Ryū Chishū

1935

32. B&W, Partial sound, Lost

An Innocent Maid

箱入り娘 *Hakoiri musume* (Literally: "Daughter in a box")

Shōchiku Kamata Studio

Story by Shikitei Sanu, Script by Noda Kōgo, Ikeda Tadao

Cinematography: Mohara Hideo

Script in existence, but no negative or prints

This was Ozu's third *Kihachi mono*, once again in Tokyo's back alleys. Kihachi lives with his son, who constantly scolds him, making rice cakes. The girl next door loves a young man, but her mother insists on marrying her off to a merchant who has been courting her. Kihachi intervenes on the wedding day, and eventually the girl marries the boy she loves, and they take the train north for their honeymoon. The film had sound but no dialogue.

Cast: Iida Chōko, Tanaka Kinuyo, Sakamoto Takeshi, Tokkan Kozō, Takeuchi Ryōichi, Aono Kiyoshi, Yoshikawa Mitsuko, Kake Shusuke, Ōyama Kenji

*

Documentary short:
鏡獅子 *Kagamijishi*
Prints in existence, 24 minutes

The film is about the kabuki theater, focusing on one of its stars at the time performing the elaborate Lion Dance, which is the title of the film. Ozu's studio asked him to make it following a request by the Ministry of Education which intended the film to be shown abroad. The film has full sound; it begins with narration about the actor and the dance, and then music and singing accompany the performance.[2]

*

33. B&W, Partly sound (music)
An Inn in Tokyo
東京の宿 *Tōkyō no yado*

Shōchiku Kamata Studio
Story by "Winthat Monnet" (Ozu, Ikeda and Arata), Script by Ikeda Tadao and Arata Masao
Cinematography: Mohara Hideo
Music: Horiuchi Keizō
Running time: 80 minutes
Number nine on the *Kinema Jumpo* list

2. See also Bordwell, *Ozu and the Poetics of Cinema*, 261.

Pre-Neo-Realism?

The fourth and last *Kihachi mono* goes back more or less to where the "series" began, although this time Kihachi has two small boys, and is unemployed. With the children in tow, he goes looking for work in a foreboding industrial landscape but is rejected at every plant. They meet with a woman, Otaka, and her little girl, who are also homeless, and spend the nights in a cheap inn for the poor. On the evening of the third day Kihachi runs into Otsune, an old acquaintance who owns a restaurant and who helps him find a job. He gets Otsune to also help Otaka and her daughter, but after a week when all goes well, Kihachi is shocked to find Otaka working in a saké bar; he thought she was above such an occupation. Crying, she tells him she had to do it because her daughter is ill with dysentery and she needs to pay the hospital bill. He tells her to go back to her daughter, and after failing to borrow the money from Otsune, determines implausibly to steal it. He sends his boys with the money to the hospital, and while evading the police goes to see Otsune to ask her to take care of his children, before he sets out to give himself up at the police station.

Some post-war critics thought that this film resembles the later Italian genre of neo-realism, but David Bordwell explains that contrary to that genre, Ozu's film is much more structured, and differs also in other ways.[3] To viewers nowadays this film, especially its first half, may be reminiscent of another genre: the post-apocalyptic. The father and sons constantly walk in what seems almost like a desert, nothing like the familiar Tokyo. There are factories and huge gas tanks in the background, but up front, it is an empty land, devoid of trees, crisscrossed by only telegraph or electric lines. It is hot and dry, and they are hungry. There seems to be no hope for them, no way out. By a stroke of fate, their luck changes, even if only for a short while.

There are several unforgettable scenes in this film. In one, the hungry father and children fantasize on what they would like to eat. The father says he misses drinking saké most of all, and the

3. Bordwell, *Ozu and the Poetics of Cinema*, 262.

elder son mimics pouring him some into what would be a traditional small cup, which the father mimics downing. Then the son offers him his cupped hands as a larger bowl to drink from, and the father warns him not to spill any. Later in the film, Kihachi fills a large glass with saké until it spills over, and downing it resolves to get the money for Otaka no matter what.

Still, amidst all the hardships, the children manage to enjoy themselves and act like children. One night at the inn, the elder son covets an officers' cap that another child flaunts. The next day, with a little money he earned, rather than buy the needed food he buys such a cap, letting his brother and even the little girl wear it in turn. It's an act of defiance, which we can identify with and admire.

There is also a certain subtle sexual tension. When Kihachi runs into Otsune, she seems very happy to see him and to extend her help, but when Otaka appears on the scene, we can see her disappointment. And when Kihachi asks her for a loan to help Otaka, she refuses, reminding him that he still owes her money that she is willing to forgo, but will not give him any more. She cries when he goes to turn himself in. However, nothing much happens between Kihachi and Otaka. Watching the children play they say things like "the best time is as kids who know nothing," and "I wish I could be a kid again." This must reflect Ozu's feelings, as he was sometimes described as child-like by those who knew him. It is clear that he never forgot what it means to be a child, and for that reason was so successful in directing children in so many of his films.

Cast:

The opening credits list the names of six actors and their roles. Some uncredited actors were identified, and some descriptions of roles added.

Kihachi—Sakamoto Takeshi

His elder son, Zenkō—Tokkan Kozō

His younger son, Masakō—Suematsu Takayuki

Otaka—Okada Yoshiko

Her daughter—Kojima Kazuko

Otsune—Iida Chōko

Uncredited:

Policeman, answering the phone—Ryū Chishū

Policeman, coming to the house—Nishimura Seiji

1936

34. B&W, Partly sound, Lost

College is a Nice Place

大学よいとこ *Daigaku yoi toko*

Shōchiku Kamata Studio

Story by "James Maki," Script by Arata Masao

Cinematography: Mohara Hideo

Script in existence, but no negative or prints

Unlike Ozu's previous college films, comedies all, this film had a dark tone, and its title is ironic. Education seems meaningless and will not lead to secure jobs. Students cut class, and some quit before getting their degrees. One of the students is married and his wife encourages him not to give up. The students who remain in college keep up their routines but without much hope. Ryū Chishū had top billing for the first time as the student who quits school to return to the countryside.

Cast: Konoe Toshiaki, Ryū Chishū, Kobayashi Tokuji, Ōyama Kenji, Ikebe Tsurihiko, Hikabe Akira, Takasugi Sanae, Aono Kiyoshi, Iida Chōko, Izumo Yaeko, Saitō Tatsuo, Sakamoto Takeshi, Tokkan Kozō

*

From here on, all films have full sound and dialogue, and none were lost.

35. B&W
The Only Son
ひとり息子 *Hitori musuko*

Shōchiku Kamata Studio
Story by "James Maki," Script by Ikeda Tadao and Arata Masao
Cinematography: Sugimoto Shōjirō
Music: Itō Senji
Running time: 83 minutes
Number four on the *Kinema Jumpo* list

This Is Talkie

Not for the first time Ozu includes scenes from a foreign movie in his film (such as the scenes from *If I Had a Million* in *Woman of Tokyo*). This time it is a German-language film about the life of Schubert (and there are several other German references throughout the film). This is an excuse for the son in the film to tell his aging mother: "This is called talkie," thus introducing Ozu's first. Sadly for the son, who had borrowed money to entertain his mother, she keeps falling asleep.

The film opens with a maxim, a quote from writer Akutagawa Ryūnosuke that states: "The first act of the tragedy of human life begins with being a parent and a child." This maxim could have served for many other Ozu films as well. This one opens in 1923 in the remote countryside, with a widowed mother working in a silk mill while raising her only son. He does well in elementary school, so his teacher encourages the mother to allow him to get further education. The mother is reluctant, as it puts a heavy burden on her, but eventually agrees. The film then skips forward to 1935. The aged mother tells a coworker at the mill that she intends to visit her son in Tokyo, and that it's time he got married. Arriving in Tokyo she learns he is already married and has a baby son. Furthermore, they live in a remote and shabby suburb, and the son, who for a while was a civil servant, teaches night school and barely makes ends meet. At first, he seems happy to see his mother and does his best to entertain her, but gradually he admits defeat. They visit the teacher, who, full of hope, had moved to Tokyo, but now makes a living for his family of six by running a *tonkatsu* (pork-chop) restaurant. The mother chides her son for giving up, but is then impressed by his kindness when he helps a neighbor whose son was kicked by a horse. Before leaving Tokyo, the mother reveals that she has lost her home and land for her son's sake, and now lives in the factory dormitory. After she leaves, the son vows to try harder, but will he? Back home the mother puts on a good face for her friend, but the film ends with her in a posture of resignation, with the factory walls closing in on her like a prison.

One of the most memorable scenes in this film takes place in a bleak space similar to the one that dominated *An Inn in Tokyo*: empty, desert-like, with chimneys belching smoke in the background. The son tells his mother that what they are seeing is Tokyo's waste incineration plant. They sit on the ground and the son asks his mother: "What did you expect me to be? . . . You are disappointed, aren't you? . . . I haven't meant to become like this . . . ." He is trying to tell her how difficult it is to get along in the big city even with a good education, but she insists: "Your life is still ahead of you, you mustn't give up." This is so poignant because we know that the mother has sacrificed so much for her son, and that they both love and care for each other, yet can't help feeling disappointed. They keep on sitting there, listening to the larks flying and chirping in the sky above them.

In a way, this film foreshadows the celebrated *Tokyo Story*. Here, too, a parent comes from the countryside to visit an adult child in Tokyo, and is disappointed in what he has become, although later the parents say otherwise. There is even a scene in which an expensive outing is planned but has to be given up because of a sick child (here the neighbor's, in the later film, the elder son's patient). The film includes another storyline that Ozu has already used and will use again, formerly in *Tokyo Chorus* and much later in *An Automn Afternoon*: the old teacher who must make a living by keeping a modest restaurant. But regardless of what comes before or after, this film stands on its own as a beautiful and relevant work of art.

Cast:

The opening credits list the names of thirteen actors, all matched with their characters. Some further information identifying them is added.

Nonomiya Tsune (Otsune)—Iida Chōko

Her son, Nonomiya Ryōsuke—Himori Shinichi

Ryōsuke as a child—Hayama Masao

Ryōsuke's wife, Sugiko—Tsubōchi Yoshiko

Tokyo neighbor, Otaka—Yoshikawa Mitsuko

Her son, Tomibo—Tokkan Kozō

Her daughter, Kimiko—Kojima Kazuko

The teacher, Ōkubo—Ryū Chishū

His wife—Naniwa Tomoko

Their son—Bakudan Kozō

Otsune's coworker at the factory—Takamatsu Eiko

Tomibo's playmate—Katō Seiichi

Older teacher at Ryōsuke's school, Matsumura—Aono Kiyoshi

1937

36. B&W
What Did the Lady Forget?
淑女は何を忘れたか　*Shukujo wa nani o wasureta ka*

Shōchiku Ōfuna Studio
Script by Fushimi Akira and "James Maki"
Cinematography: Mohara Hideo, Atsuta Yūharu
Music: Itō Senji
Running time: 71 minutes
Number eight on the *Kinema Jumpo* list

Mocking the Bourgeoisie

After several films among working-class people, Ozu is back in high society, glimpses of which were already seen earlier (*The Lady and the Beard*, *Where Now Are the Dreams of Youth?*). The "lady" in the title, who also gets first—and rarely, an individual—billing on the credits' list, is the very proper Tokiko, who is seen spending time with a couple of woman friends of the same ilk. She is married to a professor of medicine, whom she constantly bosses around. They are visited by her niece from Osaka, Setsuko, a *moga* of whose ways Tokiko does not approve, especially when she returns home late and drunk. The husband stays overnight at his assistant Okada's place when he is supposed to be away playing golf, fearing he would run into trouble if his wife finds out. Setsuko encourages him to stand up to his wife, even to use force, and when Tokiko keeps interrogating both of them, he slaps her face once. Soon after that, both Setsuko and the husband apologize to Tokiko, but speaking the next day with her friends, she seems proud of her husband's newfound assertiveness. Setsuko, who becomes romantically involved with Okada, returns to Osaka with the intention of coming back soon, and Tokiko coyly initiates a night of marital pleasure with her husband.

Viewed today, we feel uncomfortable with the "taming of the shrew" motif, but otherwise the film is very funny, and can be regarded as an early prototype of Ozu's post-war social comedies. Here he is mocking every aspect of the bourgeoisie's manners and attitudes, and no character—save perhaps for the two schoolboys, the son of one of Tokiko's friends and his classmate, who get the upper hand over the adults—escapes Ozu's irony. On a different level, Ozu introduces certain forms of traditional Japanese entertainment, and treats them with respect. There is a kabuki play, which we can only hear while the camera is showing us the audience (this will be repeated in *Early Summer* and *The Flavor of Green Tea over Rice*), and we are treated to quite a long dance by two geishas. The camera also tracks the English inscription in the Cervantes Bar: "I drink upon occasion, sometimes upon no occasion—Don Quichotte," which will reappear in *The Munekata Sisters*. We are also treated to some arithmetic puzzles which the adults cannot solve but a boy can.

So, what did the lady forget? According to Bordwell, Tokiko "forgot to appreciate her husband, while Setsuko forgot that modern men cannot and should not behave like samurai."[4] Still, men will slap women's faces on a few other occasions in future Ozu films, but women will also slap men's faces.

Incidentally, while this and many other films are available on the Internet, the English translation supplied with many of them is often inaccurate or plainly wrong. For example, according to the English subtitles, Setsuko asks her uncle to take her to a "geisha house," but there is no such thing (geishas don't entertain their guests in their houses). What Setsuko is saying is that she would like to see some Tokyo geishas (supposedly she is already familiar with Osaka ones and wishes to compare them), and her uncle gives in and takes her to a restaurant where the geishas entertain them (the old lady who comes to thank them for their patronage is the restaurant's proprietress, as indicated in the script and opening titles). I don't know how this problem can be rectified and can only encourage caution regarding the available translations.

4. Bordwell, *Ozu and the Poetics of Cinema*, 279.

Cast:

The opening credits list the names of twenty actors, all matched with their characters. Some descriptive details are added.

A lady from Kojimachi, Tokiko—Kurishima Sumiko

Her husband, Doctor Komiya—Saitō Tatsuo

The niece from Osaka, Setsuko—Kuwano Michiko

University assistant, Okada—Sano Shūji

Ushigume executive, Sugiyama, a golfing friend of the doctor —Sakamoto Takeshi

His wife, Chiyoko, a friend of Tokiko—Iida Chōko

Mitsuko, a widow from Gotenyama, a friend of Tokiko —Yoshikawa Mitsuko

Her son, Fujio, tutored by Okada—Hayama Masao

His classmate, Tomio—Tokkan Kozō

Movie star of Ōfuna Studio, seen in the theater (himself) —Uehara Ken

Restaurant proprietress where the geisha party is held —Suzuki Utako

Fumi, the maid at the Komiya house—Izumo Yaeko

Cervantes Bar proprietress—Tachibana Yasuko

University professor—Ōyama Kenji

Tokyo geishas:

Ōtsuka Kimiyo

Naniwa Tomoko

Mizushima Mitsuyo

Kuhara Yoshiko

Komaki Kazuko

Higashiyama Mitsuko

1941

37. B&W
The Brothers and Sisters of the Toda Family
戸田家の兄妹 *Todake no kyōdai*

Shōchiku Ōfuna Studio
Script by Ikeda Tadao and Ozu
Cinematography: Atsuta Yūharu
Music: Itō Senji
Running time: 105 minutes
Number one on the *Kinema Jumpo* list (Ozu's fourth)

In Praise of Young Japan

After returning from the war in China, Ozu worked on a script titled "The Flavor of Green Tea over Rice," which was rejected by the censors on account of it not meeting wartime standards (Ozu would make a different version of it fourteen years later). His next script, although not overtly militaristic in any way, was approved and made. On the one hand it continues the mockery of the bourgeoise from the previous film, but here this theme has more than just a comic or satirical effect; a positive alternative is offered.

The film introduces the drama of the large family that will reappear in several post-war Ozu films. In this one, the affluent Todas have three daughters and two sons, the three eldest of whom are already married. The father dies suddenly on his wife's sixty-first birthday, and it turns out he had debts that make it necessary to sell the big house and many heirlooms. The mother and youngest daughter Setsuko thus lose their home, and are shunted between the households of the elder siblings, ending up in the family's dilapidated seaside villa. The second son, Shōjirō, who went to work in China, returns for the first anniversary of the father's death, and blatantly criticizes his elder brother and sisters for failing to care for the mother and Setsuko. He suggests taking them with him to China, but first Setsuko offers to arrange his marriage to her working-class friend Tokiko.

Although he is absent for a large part of the film, Shōjirō is clearly its hero. He starts as the wayward son, who used to quarrel with his father and had no clear purpose in life. He is late to the family's picture taking session, then goes fishing in Osaka without telling anyone, so is late to learn about his father's death, and appears at the wake in his everyday cloths, sneaking out to meet his friends in a restaurant. However, he eventually makes up his mind to become responsible and goes to work in Tientsin, a major Chinese port town occupied by Japan. He is also late for the father's anniversary memorial service, but now appears in some kind of uniform (without insignia), and although being the younger son, criticizes his elders severely, dismissing them one by one from the ceremonial dinner of which they were about to partake. There is a clear message here: the older generation has turned egotistical, spoiled, and unreliable, but a younger, honest, and energetic one, reasserting traditional values of filial duty, is there to lead the way forward. In the final scene, when Tokiko comes visiting, Shōjirō again sneaks out through the back and runs freely along the seashore, bursting with energy. Perhaps he is not ready to get married yet, or is just shy, but he is certainly ready to lead the way. Thus Ozu, without resorting to any form of propaganda, managed to reflect the spirit of the time, while maintaining his artistic integrity.

Besides the subject matter, the style of Ozu's future films is also confidently established here, with the "empty" shots sometimes creating a surprising transition, and the action framed between half-closed sliding doors and other "obstacles," as in the family houses of the later films. The melancholic key theme and the use of music to bridge between scenes also serves as a model for the later films. But with all its serious intent, the film does not lack flashes of typical humor, including an incredible reference to an earlier Ozu film: in *That Night's Wife*, the detective picks up a fedora hat to demonstrate to the wife that he is aware of her husband hiding in the apartment, then casually puts it on her head. Now, first we see lines of hats outside the hall where the wake for the father is taking place, and then Shōjirō, arriving late as usual, tells Setsuko there's no use crying, placing his hat on her head in a similar gesture to the detective's, which here seems totally out of context, but in fact is characteristic of Shōjirō, and of Ozu's playful ways.

The cast includes many of Ozu's regular actors since the 1920's, but also some new faces that will be part of the post-war generation of his "family," including the reliable Miyake Kuniko, but most of all Saburi Shin in the role of Shōjirō. Saburi was well known as one of the three big male stars of Shōchiku at the time, the other two being Sano Shūji, who was in the previous film and will reappear in subsequent ones, and Uehara Ken, who was also in the previous film, in a short cameo as himself. The young Saburi has a magnetic presence in this film, somewhat lighter in tone than in the later films, where he is more respectable and subdued. Included also are several contemporary female stars, such as—in the substantial role of Setsuko—Takamine Mieko in her first and only appearance in an Ozu film, and playing her friend Tokiko, Kuwano Michiko in her second and last. The film enjoyed not only critical success, which Ozu had already known several times before, but was also a huge popular success, which for him was rare.

Cast:

The opening credits list the names of twenty-eight actors, all matched with their characters. They are presented below in a partially different order, with some further details added from the script.

The father, Toda Shintarō—Fujino Hideo

The mother—Katsuragi Fumiko

The eldest daughter, Chizuru—Yoshikawa Mitsuko

Her son, Asai Ryōkichi—Hayama Masao

The elder son, Shinichirō—Saitō Tatsuo

His wife, Kazuko—Miyake Kuniko

Their daughter, Mitsuko—Takagi Mayuko

The second son, Shōjirō—Saburi Shin

The second daughter, Ayako—Tsubōchi Yoshiko

Her husband, Mr. Amamiya—Konoe Toshiaki

The third daughter, Setsuko—Takamine Mieko

Setsuko's friend, Tokiko—Kuwano Michiko

The family's old maid, Kiyo—Iida Chōko

The father's secretary, Mr. Suzuki—Kawamura Reikichi

Eel restaurant proprietress—Okamura Fumiko

Friends of Shōjirō:

Inoue—Ryū Chishū

Uchida—Yamaguchi Isamu

Antique dealers:

Sakamoto Takeshi

Nishimura Seiji

Photographer—Tani Reikō

Kazuko's visiting friend, Mrs. Tanimoto—Morikawa Masami

Her accompanying friends:

Wakamizu Kinuko

Shinobu Setsuko

Young maids in various houses:

At Chizuru's, Take—Fumiya Chiyoko

At Chizuru's, Shige—Izumo Yaeko

At Shinichirō's, Kane—Okamoto Eiko

At Ayako's, Kinu—Kōno Toshiko

Officiating at the wake, Mr. Hatakeyama—Takeda Shunrō

1942

38. B&W
There was a Father
父ありき　*Chichi ariki*

Shōchiku Ōfuna Studio
Script by Ikeda Tadao, Yanai Takao and Ozu
Cinematography: Atsuta Yūharu
Music: Saiki Kyōichi
Running time: 87 minutes
Number two on the *Kinema Jumpo* list

Father Is Back

After the previous film in which the younger generation was given the upper hand, we are suddenly back with the father as the pillar of society. Still, he can also be said to be stepping off the stage ("There *was* a Father"), after preparing the way for the young, but the patriarchal viewpoint informs this film deeply, and—unprecedented for Ozu—feminine presence is minimal.

The film covers a period of about fifteen years. We first meet Mr. Horikawa, the widowed school teacher, as he raises his elementary school-aged son, Ryōhei, in Kanazawa. Horikawa leads his class on a school excursion to Tokyo (not seen), Kamakura, and finally Hakone, where a student drowns in a boat accident. Horikawa takes full responsibility, resigning his position and telling a colleague that he can no longer trust himself to assume responsibility for the lives of his students. He first moves with Ryōhei to his hometown of Ueda in Nagano, but needing a better income to support his son's education, he goes to Tokyo in search of a job, leaving Ryōhei in a school dormitory. The separation is very painful for Ryōhei, but his father insists, then and later, that striving for excellence and fulfilling one's duty must take precedence over personal feelings. Horikawa works as a supervisor in a Tokyo factory, and we learn about Ryōhei's graduation from high school, and later from college, then of his becoming a teacher in Akita (in northern Honshu, where he had been studying). Father and son meet for a short vacation at a spa, and Ryōhei expresses his wish for them to be united in Tokyo, but Horikawa once again lectures him about duty. Ryōhei does come to Tokyo eventually for his physical conscription examination and stays for a few days with his father, who goes to a class-reunion party organized by his former students. That night the father offers to arrange his son's engagement to Fumiko, the daughter of his former colleague, Hirata, but the following morning he suffers a stroke. On his deathbed he manages to remind Ryōhei to honor his duty and to ask Fumiko to take care of him. In the last scene, Ryōhei and Fumiko are on the train back north, bearing the father's ashes.

This is probably the most serious and didactic among all of Ozu's films, previous or later. Released when the Pacific War was already raging and the film industry was shackled by national ideology and heavy censorship, Ozu, too, showed his commitment to the spirit of the time and the superiority of Japanese culture. But there are several reasons why we can still enjoy this film today without too much cringing. Ozu doesn't fail to keep his commitment to his own art, so the film is beautifully shot and constructed in his familiar style, and it does not demonstrate any overt militarism. Further, the film emphasizes Buddhism rather than State Shinto, the "national religion" of Japan, and it contains all kinds of little things that allow us to enjoy it in spite of the strong message. For example, Ozu offers us reminders of his previous films, sometimes even with a little wink. On the blackboard in the father's class, there is a mathematical problem very similar to the one seen in the classroom of *The Only Son*. There are two scenes where the father and son are fishing, acting in unison just like the father and son in *Story of Floating Weeds*. More playfully, when the father returns home drunk after the class-reunion party, he asks for a glass of water, as did the drunk father in *The Brothers and Sisters of the Toda Family*; however, *that* father collapses in front of our eyes before he gets the water, while *this* father is fine, offering to arrange his son's engagement. He collapses the next morning, off screen, although we witness his deterioration when his son rushes to his side. And how about this joke: when the father tells Ryōhei that he'll be moving to the school in Ueda, the son consoles himself by saying that at least there the children don't know that his father was nicknamed "badger" and that the kids used to call him "little badger," but when his father visits him in his next school, the children suggest finding a nickname for him, offering "badger" as if it were the obvious choice. Finally, although by this time English was frowned upon as the language of the enemy, we still get a glimpse of a schoolboy practicing it and complaining about it being tedious (if "hen" is a female chicken and "cock" is male, what is "dog"?).

And after appearing in almost all of Ozu's previous films in small or supporting roles, Ryū Chishū finally landed the leading role, and what a great job he made of it. His gradual aging throughout the film is so credible, that we might believe it was actually taking place. Everything that he goes on to project in his great post-war roles is already here. If for nothing else, this film deserves repeated watching due to this great actor in his prime.

Cast:

The opening credits list the names of twenty-eight actors, all matched with their characters. They are listed below in a different order, closer to when they first appear on the screen, with some further details added.

The father, Horikawa Shūhei—Ryū Chishū

His son, Ryōhei—Sano Shūji

Ryōhei as a child—Tsuda Haruhiko

Students of the Hokuriku Middle School in Kanazawa, where the father teaches:

Ōsugi Tsuneo

Hayama Masao

Nagai Tatsurō

Fujimatsu Shōtarō

Teachers on the school trip:

Kawara Kanji

Kurata Yūsuke

Photographer in Kamakura—Mozuka Morihiko

Hirata Makoto, a teacher in Kanazawa, later met in Tokyo—Sakamoto Takeshi

His daughter, Fumiko—Mito Mitsuko

His son, Seiichi—Ōtsuka Masayoshi

Priest with whom the father stays in Ueda—Nishimura Seiji

Employee in the Tokyo factory- Miyajima Kenichi

Students of the Tohoku Industrial School where the son teaches:

Kofujita Shōichi

Ogata Shōichi

Yokoyama Jun

Okita Giichi

Graduates who hold a party for their teachers:

Kurokawa Yasutarō—Saburi Shin

Uchida Minoru—Himori Shinichi

Ōyama Kenji

Mitsui Kōji

Kisaragi Teruo

Kubota Katsumi

Maid at Horikawa's home—Fumiya Chiyoko

Doctor at hospital—Nara Shinyō

Note:

The credits also include "Teacher of *kanbun*—Tani Reikō," but I was unable to spot Tani anywhere in the film. According to the script, scene seventeen occurs back at the school after the accident, and a *kanbun* class is taking place, but it must have been cut in the surviving copies. It is obvious that some material is missing at the end or the beginning of a few of the film's reels, where there are sudden abrupt jumps forward. Also, comparing the surviving script with the film, it is evident that some other scenes were cut out, presumably when the film was rereleased after the war. The last part of scene sixty nine, in which the father sings a Chinese song at the class reunion, is also missing. So, in fact, this one could also be considered as one of Ozu's partially lost films, although it is not so designated.

1947

39. B&W
Record of a Tenement Gentleman
長屋紳士録 *Nagaya shinshiroku* (Better title: "A Who's Who of the Tenements")

Shōchiku Ōfuna Studio
Script by Ozu and Ikeda Tadao
Cinematography: Atsuta Yūharu
Music: Saitō Ichirō
Running time: 72 minutes
Number four on the *Kinema Jumpo* list

Post-War Realities

Ozu's first post-war film reflects some of the harsh realities of the time: rationing, scavenging, barter, and homeless war orphans. It also recalls Ozu's pre-war films, in particular the *Kihachi mono*, and more specifically, *Passing Fancy*.

The film is relatively short, and its protagonist is Otane, a widowed and childless shopkeeper. A lost boy is thrust upon her, and at first, she does all she can to get rid of him, but after a few days she softens and becomes attached to the taciturn child. She buys him some new clothes and takes him to the zoo and to have their picture taken. But just then the boy's father, who has been looking for him everywhere, appears at her home and she must part with the boy, but resolves to find and adopt another one.

One of the most outrageous sequences in the film, demonstrating Ozu's inexhaustive ability to reinvent his art, occurs when Otane takes the boy to have their joint portrait photographed in a studio. As usual with Ozu, the preparation is long, but after the photographer presses the shutter of the large camera, there is suddenly a cut to darkness, leaving us confused until the upside-down image of the couple, as seen through the old camera's lens, appears. We are relieved, but then there is an even longer cut to darkness. Is something wrong with the film? We can still hear them speaking in the background. Then it looks like a curtain is being lifted, and we see the studio, now empty. In his subtle manner, Ozu always finds new ways to surprise and even startle his viewers, and we enjoy it all very much.

The reliable ensemble of Ozu's pre-war actors is here once again, some of them for the last time. These include Iida Chōko, Ozu's most constant actress since his earliest films, usually in supporting roles, but here in the leading role of Otane, expressing a wide range of emotions and moods. Sakamoto Takeshi is Kihachi once again, although a true patriarch this time. Ryū Chishū gives one of his delightful reciting performances.

The exact way in which this unassuming film is planned and executed caused David Bordwell to make this astounding comment: "If Ozu had made only this seventy-two minute film, he would have to be considered one of the world's great directors."[5]

Cast:

The opening credits list the names of fourteen actors, all matched with their characters. Some descriptive details are added.

5. Bordwell, *Ozu and the Poetics of Cinema*, 301.

Otane, a widowed shopkeeper—Iida Chōko

Kōhei, the lost boy—Aoki Hōhi

His father—Ozawa Eitarō

Kiku, Otane's friend, an elderly geisha—Yoshikawa Mitsuko

Tamekichi, a tinker– Kawamura Reikichi

His daughter, Yukiko—Mimura Hideko

Tashiro, a fortune teller—Ryū Chishū

Kawayoshi Kihachi, head of the neighborhood group, a dyer —Sakamoto Takeshi

His wife, Tome—Takamatsu Eiko

His daughter, Shigeko—Osafune Fujiyo

His son, Hei-chan—Kōno Yūichi

A woman who Otane met in Chigasaki—Tani Yoshino

Photographer—Tonoyama Taiji

Sweet shop owner, in the neighborhood meeting —Nishimura Seiji

1948

40. B&W

A Hen in the Wind

風の中の牝鶏 *Kaze no naka no mendori*

Shōchiku Ōfuna Studio

Script by Saitō Ryōsuke and Ozu

Cinematography: Atsuta Yūharu

Music: Itō Senji

Running time: 84 minutes

Number seven on the *Kinema Jumpo* list

Post-War Melodrama

Tokiko, a woman in her late twenties, is raising her young son Hiroshi while waiting for her husband Shūichi to be repatriated from the war. She supports herself as a seamstress, but must sell her kimono to survive. When Hiroshi suddenly gets sick, and she can't pay the hospital bill, in despair she prostitutes herself for one night. Her friend Akiko scolds her for not coming to her for help, but Tokiko says she couldn't ask her, as she is poor too. Soon after that, Shūichi comes back and the family is happily reunited, but when questioned by her husband, Tokiko reveals what she has done. He becomes abusive, demanding to know all the details, and finally rapes her. Although he still has his pre-war job, Shūichi can't focus on work and goes to the brothel where his wife went. He talks with a young prostitute, Fusako, and decides to help her, asking his boss to find her employment. His boss asks why he can be forgiving towards the young prostitute but can't forgive his wife. Returning home, he is still angry, and when arguing with Tokiko pushes her and she falls down the stairs. Tokiko climbs back painfully without his help. The two finally reconcile, deciding to put the past behind them and start afresh.

Donald Richie quotes Ozu, who wrote about this film ten years after it was made: "Well, everyone has his failures. There are all kinds of failures, however, and some of my failures I like. This film is a bad failure."[6] One tends to agree, although the director may have been a bit too harsh with himself. Indeed, this is probably Ozu's least pleasing film since the mid 1930's and to the end of his career (although *The Munakata Sisters* may vie for the same position). Still, it must not be ignored, and David Bordwell finds various reasons to treat it as seriously as he treats the other films.

Untypically of Ozu, even in his most serious films, there is hardly a grain of humor in this one. However, and also atypically, critics argue whether this film should be viewed as allegorical, and if so, what is its message? Does the defilement of Tokiko symbolize the loss of national purity with Japan's defeat, while Shūichi's

6. Richie, *Ozu*, 234.

violence directed at her reflects the ingrained brutality of the war? Does the film ask the Japanese to lay down the mistakes of the past and start anew, looking forward rather than backward? It is quite possible that such an intention was on Ozu's mind when he was making this film. Viewed this way, *A Hen in the Wind* rises above the superficial level of melodrama.

Of course, the sexual content is only hinted at, never shown. In the brothel, the room in which Tokiko should be is shown empty, and then the customer is shown coming out, later talking about his ambivalent experience. The rape of Tokiko by her husband must be assumed, as hardly anything is shown except for his menacing and her submissive postures. As for the cast, two pre-war stars, Tanaka Kinuyo and Sano Shūji, are back in the leading roles, as are a few other familiar faces, and there are also some newcomers.

Cast:

The opening credits list the names of twenty actors, all matched with their characters. They are listed here in a somewhat different order, with some descriptive details added.

Amamiya Shūichi—Sano Shūji

His wife, Tokiko—Tanaka Kinuyo

Their son, Hiroshi—Nakagawa Hideto

Ida Akiko, Tokiko's friend—Murata Chieko

Noma Orie, Akiko's neighbor and a go-between for vice —Minakami Reiko

Sakai Hikozō, Tokiko's landlord—Sakamoto Takeshi

His wife, Tsune—Takamatsu Eiko

His daughter, Ayako—Osafune Fujiyo

His son, Shōichi—Aoki Hōhi

Satake Waichirō, Shūichi's employer—Ryū Chishū

Doctor—Nagao Toshinosuke

Policeman—Nakagawa Kenzō

Madam at the brothel—Okamura Fumiko

Onoda Fusako, young prostitute whom Shūichi wishes to help —Fumiya Chiyoko

Furakawa, customer at the brothel—Shimizu Ichirō

Men in the brothel:

A—Mitsui Kōji

B—Teshirogi Kunio

Nurses at the hospital:

A—Tani Yoshino

B—Izumi Keiko

C—Nakayama Sakae

1949

41. B&W

Late Spring

晩春　*Banshun*

Shōchiku Ōfuna Studio

Story: Hirotsu Kazuo, *Chichi to musume* ("Father and daughter"), Script by Noda Kōgo and Ozu

Cinematography: Atsuta Yūharu

Music: Itō Senji

Running time: 108 minutes

Number one on the *Kinema Jumpo* list (Ozu's fifth)

A Father and a Daughter

What more can be said about a film so perfect? Ozu's first post-war masterpiece brings together everything that was great in his work so far, taking it to the next level of artistic expression. In a way, this film also opens a new chapter, with the first dazzling appearance of Hara Setsuko, who would come to epitomize the Ozu heroine, particularly in combination with Ryū Chishū, who serves as the director's alter-ego in many of the post-war films. In four of her six appearances, Hara played next to Ryū (twice as her father, and once each as her father-in-law or elder brother; in her other two films he had minor roles), and together they created unforgettable performances.

The theme that will be repeated several times in the coming films—the need to marry off a daughter who is getting past the marrying age—appears here for the first time. Noriko is already twenty-seven, at a time when twenty-four was regarded as the upper limit for young women to be wed. The problem is that she has no wish to get married but prefers to go on living with her widowed father and taking care of him. The father is also in no hurry to let her go, but under pressure from his sister realizes that he must not be selfish and should think of his daughter's future. He lies to her when pretending that he intends to remarry, and she reacts almost like a betrayed wife. Even after meeting and liking her prospective groom, and agreeing to the marriage, she still tries to retreat, telling her father during their final trip together to Kyoto that she likes nothing better than staying at his side, but the father insists that she must begin a new life and gradually build her own happiness with her husband. Still, after the wedding takes place—off screen, as is usual with Ozu—the father is left feeling sad and forlorn.

Something else that the film offers, to a degree not seen in an Ozu film before or after, is the fore-fronting of traditional Japanese culture. The film opens with a formal tea ceremony. Later we are treated to a long scene in the *Nō* theater. We visit a major temple in Kamakura and are offered some breath-taking shots of two of Kyoto's famous sights: the wooden terraces at Kiyomizu-dera, a Buddhist temple, and the rock garden at Ryōan-ji Zen Temple. There is also a mysterious shot that elicited many interpretations: a vase against the background of a window and the shadow of bamboo, inserted between two shots of Noriko lying down in the traditional Kyoto inn. But the film also introduces an alternative through Noriko's friend Aya, who is divorced, independent, and lives in a Western-style house which is the complete opposite of the traditional family house in Kamakura, strewn with English books and magazines. Aya offers her guest shortbread cake and black tea, and she drinks saké in a bar. The film does not judge the two options. It should be remembered that it was made in the period when Japan was still under American occupation, and the contents of films were being monitored. It is possible that in a period when the American way may have seemed the better or at least the safest one, Ozu wanted to show that it does not necessarily contradict the traditional Japanese way (which was viewed as "feudalistic" by the American censors).

Beside Hara, this film also introduces, in the role of her aunt, the formidable Sugimura Haruko, who will give great performances in several films to come. So, in fact this film also signifies the changing of the guard, with most pre-war actors gone, and a new generation beginning to shine. And beside the regulars, there were several one-time shining stars in Ozu's films; this time it is the wonderful Tsukioka Yumeji in the role of Aya, Noriko's friend.

Cast:

The opening credits list the names of fourteen actors, all matched with their characters (also listed are eighteen members of the *Nō* theater group performing in the film, not repeated here). They are listed below with their ages and some descriptive details added according to the script.

Somiya Shūkichi (56), the father, professor at Tokyo University —Ryū Chishū

His daughter, Noriko (27)—Hara Setsuko

Noriko's friend, Kitagawa Aya (27)—Tsukioka Yumeji

The father's sister, Taguchi Masa (49)—Sugimura Haruko

Her son, Katsuyoshi (12)—Aoki Hōhi

Hattori Shōichi (35), the father's assistant—Usami Jun

The father's prospective bride, Miwa Akiko (38)—Miyake Kuniko

"Uncle," Onodera Jō (55), professor at Kyoto University —Mishima Masao

His second wife, Kiku (38)—Tsubōchi Yoshiko

His daughter, Misako (21)—Katsuragi Yōko

Takigawa Restaurant chef—Shimizu Ichirō

Hayashi Seizō (47), gardener at Somiya's house—Tanizaki Jun

His wife Shige (44), the help at Somiya's house —Takahashi Toyo

Tea ceremony teacher—Benisawa Yōko

1950

42. B&W

The Munakata Sisters

宗方姉妹　*Munakata shimai*

Shintōhō

Story by Osaragi Jirō, Script by Noda Kōgo and Ozu

Cinematography: Ohara Jōji

Music: Saitō Ichirō

Running time: 112 minutes

Number seven on the *Kinema Jumpo* list

Even Great Directors Slip Occasionally

This is the first film that Ozu directed for a studio other than his constant employer Shōchiku, and over the years it was available for viewing less often than his other films. Ozu accepted the offer to direct a film for the up-and-coming studio Shintōhō but had to agree to the story line and the performers as decided by the studio. The script was based on a novel, and Ozu claimed that he found it difficult working this way, rather than writing a script from scratch (although several other of his films were based on previous material). The result is less satisfactory than any of his other films of the 1950's and 60's.

The story is about a couple of sisters who convey—almost to a ridiculous degree—the contrast between old and new Japan. Setsuko, the elder, is extremely proper, always clad in a kimono, and rejects anything new. The bar she runs in Tokyo is financially strained, and her unemployed husband drinks and cares only for his cats. The younger sister Mariko, who lives with the couple, is almost a caricature of all that is new, expressing a distaste even for Buddhist temples. Their widowed father is absorbed in the traditional atmosphere of Kyoto and is not told of his terminal cancer. Mariko finds out that years before Setsuko loved Hiroshi, a furniture dealer from Kobe, and develops an interest in him and hatred for a woman who is trying to win him. Setsuko has to close down her bar, while her husband Mimura is deteriorating. He slaps her face viciously, and later dies in a drunken stupor. The way is open for Setsuko to join Hiroshi, but in spite of the fact that they care deeply for each other, she feels that it is not the right thing to do and rejects him.

There are many things here not seen in any other Ozu film: a man drenched in rain and dying of drink; a woman screaming; a man slapping a woman's face repeatedly (there were single slaps before, and a man slapping another man's face repeatedly); glasses thrown one after another against the wall of a bar; a couple about to kiss are interrupted by someone's appearance; and more. The only comic relief is supplied by Mariko with her antics and imitations of *benshi*, the silent film narrators.

The actors make an interesting combination of veterans, with a few new faces. Tanaka Kinuyo and Ryū Chishū appear together once again, after a long hiatus since the early 1930's. Uehara Ken, who had a cameo appearance as himself in *What Did the Lady Forget?*, has a substantial role as Hiroshi, while Takamine Hideko, who was last seen as a lively child of seven in *Tokyo Chorus* and by now was turning into Japan's top woman star, is the sparkling Mariko. Saitō Tatsuo makes a final appearance in an Ozu film, delivering a medical lecture to university students, just as he did in *What Did the Lady Forget?*, thirteen years earlier. Among the new faces who will be seen again in the coming years is Yamamura Sō, portraying the unhappy Mimura. As always with Ozu, all actors give top performances, but something in this film simply doesn't feel right.

Cast:

The opening credits list the names of fourteen actors, *not* matched with their characters. They are listed below in a somewhat different order and with their age according to the script, and some descriptive details added.

Munakata Tadachika (60), the father—Ryū Chishū

Setsuko (34), the elder sister, proprietress of Acacia Bar in Tokyo—Tanaka Kinuyo

Her husbnd (37), Mimura Ryōsuke—Yamamura Sō

Mariko (25), the younger sister—Takamine Hideko

Tashiro Hiroshi (35), owns a furniture shop in Kobe —Uehara Ken

Mashita Yoriko (32), a woman from Kobe—Takasugi Sanae

Maejima Gorōshichi (27), barman at Acacia Bar—Hori Yūji

Fujishiro Mieko (34), co-owner of Acacia Bar—Tsubōchi Yoshiko

Uchida Yuzuru (59), professor of medicine in Kyoto —Saitō Tatsuo

Sangin, master of a chip drinking place—Fujiwara Kamatari

Sangin maid, Kyo-chan—Sengoku Noriko

Sangin customer—Kawamura Reikichi

Tokyo inn maid—Horikoshi Setsuko

Hakone inn maid—Ichinomiya Atsuko

1951

43. B&W

Early Summer

麥秋 *Bakushū* (Literally: "The barley harvest season")

Shōchiku

Script by Noda Kōgo and Ozu

Cinematography: Atsuta Yūharu

Music: Itō Senji

Running time: 125 minutes

Number one on the *Kinema Jumpo* list (Ozu's sixth and final first place on the list)

Poetry in Motion

Ozu is famous—or notorious—for his static camera. In fact, in his later films he dispensed of camera movements all together (as he did with fades in and out, dissolves, and other such cinematic means), but his art did not seem to have suffered by this loss. However, when the camera *did* move, magic often happened. In *Early Summer*, Ozu still used tracking shots relatively often, and a few of those shots are truly unforgettable.

The film opens with a shot—from a static camera—of gentle waves breaking against the shore in Kamakura. We then move gradually into the house of the Mamiya family, situated not far from the shore, getting to know its seven members one by one as they go through their morning routine. The main concern of the family is soon made clear with the visit of the old rustic uncle: the need to *katazuke* the youngest daughter, Noriko, who will soon be past the marrying age. The meaning of *katazuke* that first comes to mind is "tidy up," "clear up," or "clear away," but it also means "to give, or dispose of one's daughter in marriage." Perhaps these associations of meaning do not sound as strange to the Japanese ear as they do to the foreigner's, but still, the daughter's reluctance to get disposed of by marrying the family's choice, a bachelor fourteen years her senior, is understandable. She acts independently and ends up choosing her partner without the family's consent, but her rebellion is a mild one: after all, she's marrying the neighbors' son, who was the best friend of her brother, a missing soldier, and she will join him and his little daughter in the remote countryside, where he will head a hospital ward. On deeper scrutiny, she is perhaps more "traditional" than "modern," as even her best friend Aya is surprised to realize. She also follows her heart, as would other young women in Ozu's subsequent films. Her marriage causes the household to split three ways, but that's the way of the world, and would have happened sooner or later, as the old father tells her kindly. In an earlier scene, we saw him going out of the house, stopping at a train crossing, sitting down, waiting for the train to pass, and not hurrying to get up again once it does: he realizes life is passing him by, but he accepts it with not much ado.

Much has already been written about the camera movements in this film, mostly by David Bordwell,[7] so there is no need to analyze them once again, perhaps only mention a few of them briefly: the breathtaking shot of the two sisters-in-law shown from the back on a sand dune, in which the camera seems to detach itself vertically from the hold of the earth's gravity; or the last, dizzying shot, in which the village and mountain remain solid in the middle of the frame while the camera travels over the barley fields (the original title of the film also means "barley harvest season"), echoing the sea in the first shot. These and other sequences in the film are pure poetic moments, created by a cinematic artist at his peak. But notice should also be given to how Ozu's playfulness and humor are enhanced by the use of camera movements and editing. For example, we see Noriko and her friend Aya tiptoe down the corridor in a traditional restaurant towards the camera, which tracks back as they advance; then the angle is reversed and the camera is tracking forward, but rather than seeing the two from behind as we would have expected, we find ourselves back in the family's house,

7. Bordwell, *Ozu and the Poetics of Cinema*, 319-321.

going towards the kitchen. This method of cutting and editing was already used once earlier in the film and will be used again even in some of the later films. From the cinematic point of view, Ozu is often master of the unexpected: he does not show us what we expect to see, but rather hides something from us, or skips forward to a different point in time or space. In the above example, what we expect to see but are not shown is what the two friends actually saw when they peeked into a room where the man Noriko would not marry was having dinner. Our curiosity about him is not to be satisfied. We see, instead, Noriko coming back home to a cold welcome by the family, having her solitary dinner in the kitchen, but steadfastly standing her ground.

Apart from the story, rich in humanism and relevant beyond its specific time and place, *Early Summer* can also be viewed as a historical document reflecting, sometimes inadvertently, the reality of life in post-war Japan. Almost every scene in the film contains treasures of social information. For example, reflecting on the old uncle's previous visit, which took place a few years earlier, not long after the end of the war, Fumiko tells her sister-in-law Noriko, "I was still wearing *monpe* then," referring to the baggy work pants that women had to wear during that period of austerity. By now, six years after the war ended, the situation has improved considerably, and women can once again wear *kimono* or skirts, and occasionally even indulge in shortbread cake, in spite of its prohibitive price. Later, in one of the last scenes, Aya warns Noriko that if she indeed goes with her chosen spouse to Akita up north, she would have to wear *monpe*: apparently, the remote, rustic parts of the country were not yet enjoying the new-found prosperity of Tokyo. But Noriko says she certainly will wear them, demonstrating once again her resolution to persevere on the path she has chosen, even if it means giving up all luxuries of modern life in the big city for the sake of accompanying the man with whom she believes she could be happy. Many more such instructive moments occur in this great film.

Among Ozu's films, *Tokyo Story* is usually considered his greatest masterpiece, appearing on various lists of "Ten Greatest

Films" and the like, but *Early Summer* is a masterpiece of no lesser quality, and in some cinematic and thematic aspects is even richer than the more famous film. I tend to regard Ozu's oeuvre as a unity, but when pressed to name his best realized or most representative films, *Early Summer* will always come to mind as one of his greatest achievements.

Cast:

Actors and characters, twenty-four in number, are matched on the film's opening credits, but in a different order than the one presented below. Characters' age is given according to the script, and some further identifying details are added.

The grandfather, Mamiya Shūkichi (68), a retired botanist —Sugai Ichirō

The grandmother, Shige (60)—Higashiyama Chieko

Elder son, Kōichi (38), a medical doctor—Ryū Chishū

Kōichi's wife, Fumiko (35)—Miyake Kuniko

Their elder son, Minoru (12)—Murase Zen

Their second son, Isamu (6)—Shirosawa Isao

The daughter, Noriko (28), an English typist at a Tokyo firm —Hara Setsuko

The old uncle, Mokichi (73)—Takadō Kuninori

Noriko's friend, Tamura Aya (28)—Awashima Chikage

Aya's mother Nobu (52), Tamura Restaurant proprietress—Takahashi Toyo

Noriko's boss, "the director" ("Semmu-san"), Satake Sōtarō (39) —Sano Shūji

Yabe Kenkichi (34), a widower and medical doctor—Nihonyanagi Hiroshi

His mother, Yabe Tami (54)—Sugimura Haruko

His daughter, Mitsuko (3)—Itō Kazuyo

Neighborhood doctor, Nishiwaki (40)—Miyaguchi Seiji

His wife, Nishiwaki Tomiko (36)—Yamamoto Tami

Noriko's married friend, Yasuda Takako ("Otaka") (28) —Igawa Kuniko

Noriko's other married friend, Takanashi Mari (28) —Shiga Matsuko

Waitress at Takigawa restaurant (where Kōichi, Fumiko and Noriko eat)—Tani Yoshino

Waitress at Tamura restaurant—Tashiro Yoshiko

Hospital nurse (announcing Aya's mother)—Terada Kayoko

Hospital assistant (calling Kōichi to the phone)—Hasebe Tomoka

Receptionist at Noriko's office (announcing Tami)—Yamada Eiko

Photographer—Tanizaki Jun

Note:

Appearing here are many members of Ozu's faithful cast, who have appeared, or will appear, more or less regularly in his films of this period. I do feel, though, that there was one miscasting in this film, and that is of Sugai Ichirō in the role of the grandfather. Sugai gives a very good performance, but he was forty-four years old when the film was made, and he sometimes looks too young for the sixty-eight year-old character he is supposed to portray. In *Tokyo Story*, Ryū Chishū will give a much more convincing performance as a man considerably older than he actually was.

1952

44. B&W

The Flavor of Green Tea over Rice

お茶漬けの味　*Ochazuke no aji*　(Literally: "The taste of *ochazuke*")

Shōchiku
Script by Noda Kōgo and Ozu
Cinematography: Atsuta Yūharu
Music: Saitō Ichirō
Running time: 116 minutes

Trains and Cars and Planes

There is no hiding the embarrassing truth: Japanese filmmakers are simply in love with trains. You would be hard pressed to find a *gendaigeki* (contemporary) Japanese film which does not include a train scene, and one even gets the impression that they would have loved to incorporate such scenes into the *jidaigeki* (historical, or samurai films) if they only could. Ozu is no exception. Train-station scenes, train-riding scenes, trains seen from a distance, trains approaching or departing—you name it, he's got it in almost every film. True, this is not a uniquely Japanese phenomenon, except for the degree of commitment. In many parts of the world, trains gained a certain poetic quality as harbingers of change in human life, and are depicted this way in art and literature. In Ozu's films, too, trains often signify a change in the life or in the consciousness of the protagonists; in *Tokyo Story*, Noriko's ride back to Tokyo signifies the turning of a new leaf in her life (and it is the only train ride actually seen, although many others take place in the story); in *Equinox Flower*, the father's train journey in the last scene reflects a change of heart concerning his daughter's marriage. Such is the case in *The Flavor of Green Tea over Rice* as well.

But not only trains: this film may be handed the locomotion first prize among all of Ozu's films. It opens with a car ride through the more scenic parts of Tokyo, followed by a train journey out of town to the resort in Suzenji, and then, uniquely among Ozu's films, an airplane is taking off, and finally there is the long and elaborate sequence of a train journey between Tokyo and Osaka, filmed from the rear observation car, and analyzed in great detail by Bordwell.[8] For the wife in the main storyline, the train signifies her means of escape from a loveless marriage, but this last-mentioned ride also shows her reflecting on her life, and the result is a change of heart and a new-found willingness to give her marriage another chance.

The film's main storyline concerns a childless upper-class couple, who seem to have very little in common. The husband, Mokichi, has simple tastes and a hands-on attitude to life; the wife, Taeko, is snobbish and willful, and probably resents the fact that she was matched with this man. The taming of the shrew takes place in a very subtle way, however, almost without the husband's intervention. It is mostly an internal process, aided perhaps by the remarks of her young niece Setsuko and her friend Aya, causing Taeko to be ashamed of the way she treats her husband, and making her realize that the fault is mainly hers.

The sub-plot in the film concerns the younger generation: Setsuko, and Mokichi's protégé nicknamed "Non-chan." They seem different from the older folks whom they sometimes despise, but are they really that different? Setsuko demonstrates willfulness of a no lesser degree than her aunt's, and the last scene indicates that if these two end up together, it's not a rose garden they'll be stepping into. "Non-chan," who seems to be ready to join the rat-race in spite of his fine words about being young and free, is very awkward in handling the girl he is attracted to. Eventually, every generation turns out to be more or less the same as the earlier one, as Ozu often seems to tell us. Basic human nature is oblivious of the passing of time.

Sandwiched between two great masterpieces—*Early Summer* the year before it and *Tokyo Story* the year following it—*The Flavor of Green Tea over Rice* is relatively lightweight, although it contains most of the well-known Ozu qualities both in form and content, including one of his most amusing scenes, showing the upper-class couple disorientated in their own kitchen. Perhaps this lightweight feeling is caused by the great amount of popular entertainment shown in it: a baseball game, a bicycle race, and the

8. Bordwell, *Ozu and the Poetics of Cinema*, 324-326.

new craze of *pachinko* that swept Japan at the time and became one of its most typical and ubiquitous institutions. The only traditional Japanese entertainment in the film is a Kabuki play, which, exactly like in *What Did the Lady Forget?* and *Early Summer*, is heard but not seen, with the camera going through the audience and focusing on some of the characters who are sitting in a box (in this case, the hapless suitor, given the slip by Setsuko). Also, between two films about relatively lower-middle-class families, here we are once again with the upper-middle-class and above, as in *What Did The Lady Forget?*, from which some scenes were lifted into this film, and *The Brothers And Sisters Of The Toda Family*, in which Saburi Shin portrayed the young and spirited brother, reappearing here once again as a ten-year older version of himself, and will reappear again in later films as a father, having advanced also to the level of a senior executive.

Speaking of actors, in this film, Ozu's main actor Ryū Chishū plays a relatively small part, as a pachinko parlor owner who turns out to be a former soldier who served under Mokichi in Singapore. He reminisces fondly about that period—probably reflecting some of Ozu's own experiences—and even bursts into a sentimental song. Mokichi is unphased; for him the war is nothing to get sentimental about, although he can't put it completely out of his mind. As often with Ozu, this motif will be picked up again later, in Ozu's very last film, *An Autumn Afternoon*; in this film, Ryū Chishū plays the erstwhile commander, and the man who served under him (in the navy, in this case), a mechanic, is the one waxing lyrical about the good old times in the war. Ozu was never shy about using old material time and again, each time giving it some new twist. This familiarity is one of the qualities that make Ozu's films so dear to the admirers of his work.

Cast:

Actors and characters, twenty-four in all, are matched on the film's opening credits, but in a different order than the one offered below. Characters' age is given according to the script, and some further identifying details are added.

The husband, Satake Mokichi (42)—Saburi Shin

His wife, Taeko (32)—Kogure Michiyo

Yamauchi Naosuke, Taeko's father (67)—Yanagi Eijirō

Chizu, Taeko's sister in law (42)—Miyake Kuniko

Her daughter, Setsuko (21)—Tsujima Keiko

Her son, Kōji (6)—Shitara Kōji

Setsuko's arranged marriage prospect (seen in Kabuki) —Hasebe Tomoka

Mokichi's school-friend's young brother, Okada Noboru ("Non-chan") (26)—Tsuruta Kōji

Taeoko's friend, Amamiya Aya (31), fashion shop owner —Awashima Chikage

Aya's husband, Amamiya Tōichirō (45)—Toake Hisao

A woman from Nishi Ginza (Mr. Amamiya's companion to a ball game)—Shiga Matsuko

Taeoko's other friend, Kuroda Takako (31)—Uehara Yōko

House maid Fumi (21)—Kozono Yōko

House maid Yone (32)—Yamamoto Tami

Pachinko parlor owner, served under Mokichi in the war, Hirayama Sadao (42)—Ryū Chishū

Hirayama's wife, Shige (30)—Mochizuki Yūko

Shop girls at Aya's:

Miyama Etsuko

Hinatsu Noriko

Waitress in Echo Bar—Kitahara Mie

Company director Ogawa, Mokichi's boss (65)—Ishikawa Kinichi

His private secretary—Nagao Toshinosuke

Office girls in Mokichi's company who call him to the boss:

Yamada Eiko

Fujioka Shōichi

Elderly man—Tanizaki Jun

1953

45. B&W
Tokyo Story
東京物語 *Tōkyō monogatari*

Shōchiku
Script by Noda Kōgo and Ozu
Cinematography: Atsuta Yūharu
Music: Saitō Takanobu
Running time: 135 minutes
Number two on the *Kinema Jumpo* list

Noriko's Smile

This is the third in what became known as "the Noriko trilogy": three films in which Hara Setsuko plays a different young woman called "Noriko." These are *Late Spring* (1949), *Early Summer* (1951), and *Tokyo Story* (1953) (in between came two other films in which Hara did not participate). In all three films she plays a modern young woman: dressed in western clothes (while the slightly older women around her usually wear *kimono*), works in an office of a large company in Tokyo (in the two later films), and seems confident and self-reliant. In the first two films, she turns out to be a little more traditional than expected: in *Late Spring*, she agrees to an arranged marriage, in spite of her personal preferences; in *Early Summer*, she displays independence by choosing her spouse against her family's wishes, but in fact she marries the boy next door, preferring to go to the backward countryside with a poor doctor she likes, over life in the modern city with a rich businessman she doesn't trust. In *Tokyo Story*, it is the other way around: she seems extremely traditional to begin with, loyal beyond measure to her old parents-in-law, but she eventually confesses to being selfish, no longer thinking constantly about her dead husband but rather about her own life and what would become of her.

Tokyo Story is usually regarded as Ozu's greatest masterpiece or most representative film. For those who know his films well, and regard his entire oeuvre as one unity, it is probably just one in a series of truly great films. Still, one cannot deny the variety of deep human feelings displayed in this particular film, as well as the amazing performances of the whole wonderful cast. Ryū Chishū gives here arguably his greatest performance as the old father (about twenty years older than his actual age at the time; the actress who plays his wife in this film played his mother in *Early Summer* two years earlier), and Hara Setsuko, too, has one of her most memorable roles. And Ozu, as always, keeps surprising us with what he does and does not show. For example, there are many train rides in the story, but only one is actually shown, towards the end of the film, when Noriko goes back to Tokyo after opening her heart to her father-in-law and receiving his blessing and encouragement to start a new chapter in her life. While on the train, she takes out the watch that belonged to her late mother-in-law and was given to her as a memento; she opens the lid of the old-fashioned watch, reflecting nostalgically on the past, and then she closes the lid back, looking forward to her life from now on. This is a very typical conclusion to an Ozu film: every ending—even one involving death—is another beginning.

While Noriko seems the paragon of filial piety, the old couple's own children are depicted mostly as the complete opposite: cold, selfish, and self-absorbed. But as with Noriko, the depiction is not totally black or white. These grown-up children must fend for themselves and their own families. The father's old friend, when drunk, complains about his own son, who has given up and makes no effort to progress in life; Hirayama's children, on the other hand, strive constantly. Kōichi is dedicated to his patients, and Shige to her business; they cannot let go. And they are not emotionally sterile either; Shige even displays true sorrow over her mother's death (although one can't help wishing that she had been a little kinder to her in life). The old parents conclude that they are lucky since their children have turned out better than average, and although they may say so mostly to comfort themselves, we can also see the grain of truth in that statement.

Perhaps the parent-child relationship could be explored from another angle as well. Shige brings up childhood grievances: her mother embarrassed her at school, and her father was often drunk. Her current attitude may have something to do with what she had to endure. Perhaps their son- and daughter-in-law are kinder to the old couple because they did not have to grow up with them as their own children did. As we know from every culture and every period, families can be hell. So, while they are expected to treat their old parents with respect, the grown-up children cannot be expected to be totally free of the sediments of the past.

Unfortunately, the original negative of *Tokyo Story* was lost in a fire, and for decades we had to do with second-rate copies. Luckily, digital restoration has brought the film back to its original beauty, or as nearly so as possible. As we watch it again and again, many scenes linger in memory, and above all Noriko's warm, accepting smile when speaking with her young sister-in-law: Yes, life is disappointing, but that is all we've got. Once again, human reality is reflected, both brilliantly and modestly, through Ozu's incomparable art.

Cast:

The opening credits list the names of thirty actors matched with their characters, including those in very small roles. They are given below in a different order than on the credits, with characters' age and some further identifying details added according to the script.

The old father, Hirayama Shūkichi (70)—Ryū Chishū

His wife, Tomi (67)—Higashiyama Chieko

Hirayama's elder son, Kōichi (47), a medical doctor —Yamamura Sō

His wife, Fumiko (39)—Miyake Kuniko

Their elder son, Minoru (14)—Murase Zen

Their second son, Isamu (6)—Mōri Mitsuhiro

Hirayama's elder daughter, Shige (44), a beautician —Sugimura Haruko

Her husband, Kaneko Kurazō (49)—Nakamura Nobuo

Her assistant, Kiyo—Annan Junko

Noriko (28), the widow of Hirayama's second son Shōji —Hara Setsuko

Hirayama's third son, Keizō (27), works for the train company in Osaka—Ōsaka Shirō

Hirayama's younger daughter, Kyōko (23), a school-teacher —Kagawa Kyōko

Hattori Shū (68), the father's old friend in Tokyo—Toake Hisao

His wife, Yone (60)—Nagaoka Teruko

Numata Sanpei (71), the father's other old friend who gets drunk with him—Tōno Eijirō

Young man boarding at Hattori's—Itokawa Kazuhiro

Proprietress of *oden* shop—Sakura Mutsuko

Noriko's neighbor in her apartment building—Mitani Sachiko

Keizō's co-worker at train station office—Abe Tooru

Hirayama's neighbor, passing by—Takahashi Toyo

Beauty salon customers:

Mizuki Ryōko

Togawa Yoshiko

Man calling Kōichi to his sick child—Tōyama Fumio

Policeman—Morozumi Keijirō

Noriko's company boss—Niijima Tsutomu

Noriko's office coworker—Suzuki Shōzō

Atami hotel maids:

Tashiro Yoshiko

Chichibu Haruko

Singer outside hotel—Miki Takashi

Doctor in Onomichi—Nagao Toshinosuke

1956

46. B&W
Early Spring
早春 *Shoshun*

Shōchiku
Script by Noda Kōgo and Ozu
Cinematography: Atsuta Yūharu
Music: Saitō Takanobu
Running time: 144 minutes
Number six on the *Kinema Jumpo* list

The Portrait of a Couple and a Generation

Out of Ozu's fifteen post-war films, nine or ten can be said to focus on the relations of parents and their grown-up children (of which seven concern, mainly or partially, the marrying off of a daughter), giving the impression that this was his "only" subject, as some critics have written.[9] However, even disregarding his pre-war films, which had several other concerns, his post-war films also show his interest in a variety of human relations and social conditions. Two almost consecutive films focus on the relationship of childless couples, of markedly different backgrounds: *The Flavor of Green Tea Over Rice* and *Early Spring*.

Unlike the very affluent couple in the former film, the couple in this one belongs to the lower middle class, which was an emerging class in Japan of that period. However, in both films the couple, after experiencing what seems to be total estrangement, are eventually reconciled. This happens mainly because the wife takes the necessary extra step. In *The Flavor of Green Tea Over Rice*, which is more comical in tone, the wife admits she was wrong, and is willing to adapt to her husband's simpler tastes. He hasn't changed,

9. See, for example, Richie, *Ozu*, 1.

but she has; he was always the wiser grown-up, while she is growing up out of her childishness in front of our eyes. In *Early Spring*, which is much more somber in tone (the difficulties between the husband and wife involve infidelity on his side, and the memory of a dead child), it is the other way around: the wife, Masako, is the adult, while the husband, Shōji, is the childish spouse. Only when Shōji gives up his lover and accepts a more challenging job in a remote place, away from his familiar social circle, is Masako willing to forgive him and give their marriage another chance. This comparison between the two films is one example of the great variety in human nuances to be found in Ozu's films, in spite of all the similarities that often stand out.

This film is Ozu's longest, with the greatest number of characters, large and small. Ozu's aim was not only to portray a couple, but to relate to the concerns of a generation, of those who came of age during or soon after the war, experiencing their "early spring." Some of them served in the army, and still maintain their attachment to their comrades. All are working hard for the rebuilding of a devastated nation (this is not something that Ozu actually tells us, but we know it to be part of their reality), but they simultaneously have very private concerns, and are all searching for love, friendship, and entertainment, as well as for purpose and meaning. Ozu portrays their lives in great detail, giving, as always, the impression that he really cares about them, and that he wishes us to sympathize with them as well. All this Ozu does in his usual tightly controlled style, with very few melodramatic moments. Even the potentially most melodramatic ones, when Shōji is confronted by his neglected lover Chiyo or by his offended wife Masako, are cut down to the bare minimum.

The actors all do a fine job, in particular the leading couple. Dashing Ikebe Ryō, who was a great star of the Japanese cinema of the 1950's and 60's, and who makes here his only appearance in an Ozu film, gives a solid portrayal of the somewhat disgruntled war veteran, who is not sure how he can improve his life (born in 1918, Ikebe himself had a long military experience in the Pacific War). Awashima Chikage, who gave sparkling comic performances in two earlier Ozu films, here plays the deep, greatly controlled role of the dejected wife who is willing to forgive. Up-and-coming star Kishi Keiko also gives an emotional but controlled performance—her only one in Ozu's films, regrettably—as the lover, Chiyo. Several Ozu regulars, and many new faces, give a variety of solid performances.

This complex film is a portrayal of both a marriage and a generation. Beyond the distance in time and place, we can still identify with those basic human feelings and hopes that never change.

Cast:

There are fifty names of actors on the opening credits, but they are *not* matched with their characters, and some have not been identified yet (a few I was able to match by identifying them in other films). Ages of characters, some names, and additional information are given according to the script.

Sugiyama Shōji (33), a company employee (*salaryman*) in Tokyo—Ikebe Ryō

His wife, Masako (30)—Awashima Chikage

Her mother, Kitagawa Shige (56), proprietress of a restaurant—Urabe Kumeko

Her younger brother, Kitagawa Kōichi (21), a student—Taura Masami

Kaneko Chiyo (nicknamed "Goldfish"), typist, Shōji's lover —Kishi Keiko

The Sugiyamas' neighbor across the alley, Tamura Seiichirō (52) —Miyaguchi Seiji

His wife, Tamura Tamako (45)—Sugimura Haruko

Arakawa (52), company deaprtment head, Shōji's boss —Nakamura Nobuo

Onodera Kiichi (45), Sugiyama's family friend, widower, employed by the same company in Ōtsu—Ryū Chishū

His son—Murase Zen

Kawai Yutaka, "Blue Mountain" café/bar owner, who used to work for the same company—Yamamura Sō

His wife, Yukiko—Miyake Kuniko

Hattori Tōkichi, customer in "Blue Mountain"—Tōno Eijirō

"Sugai no Tsū-san," customer in Shige's restaurant —Sugawara Tsūsai

Another customer at Shige's restaurant—Takeda Norikazu

Tominaga Sakae (30), widowed friend of Masako —Nakakita Chieko

War time friends of Shōji:

Hirayama—Mitsui Kōji

Sakamoto—Katō Daisuke

Several others

Miura Yūzō, Shōji's colleague, seriously ill—Masuda Junji

His mother, Sato (63)—Nagaoka Teruko

Shōji's playmates (they commute by train together, go hiking and meet in the evenings):

Aoki Taizō ("Non-chan")—Takahashi Teiji

His wife, Terumi—Fujino Takako

Tanabe ("Raigyo"/ Snakehead fish, the group usually meets at his apartment)—Suga Fujio

Nomura—Tanaka Haruo

Tsuji—Morozumi Keijirō

Honda Hisako ("Chāko")—Yamamoto Kazuko

Kimura Ichiko ("Pinko") (also seen with an eye patch) —Kawaguchi Nobu

?—Tanaka Mariko (very short hair)

Fujii ("Noppo")

Hasegawa

Shōji's co-workers:

Takagi, sits next to him—Oni Shōsuke

Okazaki, union member—Nagai Tatsurō

Other office colleagues: Hayashi, Andō, Kawaguchi, Kimura, and others

Yamada Yoshikazu

Sugita Hiroko

Shimamura Toshio

Tanizaki Jun

Hasebe Tomoka

Suenaga Isao

Nangō Yūji

Sasaki Tsuneko

Chimura Yōko

Sahara Yasushi

Inagawa Zenichi

Imai Kentarō

Matsuno Hideo

Mine Hisako

Suzuki Yasuyuki

Kanō Takako

Inoue Masahiko

Chiba Akira

Yamamoto Tami

Ōta Chieko

Nakayama Junji

1957

47. B&W
Tokyo Twilight
東京暮色 *Tōkyō boshoku*

Shōchiku
Script by Noda Kōgo and Ozu
Cinematography: Atsuta Yūharu
Music: Saitō Takanobu
Running time: 141 minutes

In Dark Tokyo

Of all Ozu's post-war films, this is the only one taking place in winter, and the constant cold adds to the gloomy atmosphere. Almost all outside scenes take place in the dark, and interior scenes are not much brighter. There is no pleasant scenery, no pleasing Japanese art, and no humor. It is the most atypical Ozu film, but in no way is it negligible.

Mr. Sugiyama is a middle-aged bank employee whom, it turns out, has been deserted by his wife in favor of his underling before the war, leaving behind three young children, one of whom since died in an accident. The elder daughter, Takako, leaves her abusive and drunk husband and comes with her two-year old daughter to stay in her father's house. The younger daughter, Akiko, a student, is in trouble. She can't get hold of her elusive boyfriend, and is trying to borrow money behind her father's back. Eventually, she has an abortion. Meanwhile it turns out that the girls' mother lives in the vicinity, managing a mahjong parlor with her third husband (the second had died during the war). Takako warns her to stay away, and Akiko starts to believe she is not her father's daughter. In distress, she is hit by a train, but it is not clear whether this was an accident or a suicide. On her deathbed she says she doesn't want to die. The mother, still shunned by her remaining daughter, moves with her husband to Hokkaido, and Takako goes back to her husband, to give her marriage a second chance. The father is left alone.

What is this film about? The focus seems to be on Akiko and her generation, and the film also deals with mother-daughter and man-woman relationships. But according to Ozu's puzzling remark, the film was about the father,[10] as many of his other films were, and perhaps we can see what he meant. The film opens with the father visiting a bar and hearing from the proprietress that his son-in-law was there recently, extremely drunk. On returning home he finds his elder daughter Takako there, having escaped from her abusive husband with her little daughter. He soon goes to see his son-in-law, and on returning home apologizes to Takako for making her marry this man rather than the one she liked better. It isn't easy for a middle-aged father to admit such a mistake and apologize to his daughter, and we can appreciate his humanity. Still, when he hears about his younger daughter Akiko having been taken to a police station, he is angry to such a degree that he says "You are no daughter of mine," which he surely regrets later. After Akiko's death and Takako and her daughter's departure he is left alone, but when he goes to work in the morning, we are treated to the first bright daylight scene of the film, which is also the final one.

According to Noda Kōgo's daughter, Ozu was frustrated by the refusal of his long-time collaborator to help him with this script (for which both of them are credited). Apparently, Noda didn't like the change of tone, and eventually both he and Ozu considered the film a failure. However, we can still appreciate the fact that like the preceding one, this film gives voice to the younger generation, and that in being so different from Ozu's other films, it is interesting in a special way. In fact, it was the last film in which Ozu experimented with new subject matter; his subsequent films—all in color, all wonderful—tread a more familiar ground.

Both Ryū Chishū and Hara Setsuko, playing a father and a daughter once again, give here perhaps their most subdued appearances. Many faces familiar from the previous film and some earlier ones are seen here again, besides several new ones,

10. Bordwell, *Ozu and the Potics of Cinema*, 341.

including, in the role of Akiko, Arima Ineko, who will play the "difficult" daughter in the next film as well. The estranged mother is played by Yamada Isuzu, one of the most decorated actresses in Japanese film history, whose career spanned 70 years, but who was in an Ozu film only this once.

Cast:

The opening credits list the names of forty-seven actors, all matched with their characters. They are given below in a different order, with characters' age and some further identifying details added according to the script.

Sugiyama Shūkichi (57), a bank auditor—Ryū Chishū

His elder daughter, Numata Takako (32)—Hara Setsuko

Her husband, Numata Yasuo (41), university teacher—Shin Kinzō

Her daughter, Numata Michiko (2)—Mori Noriko

His younger daughter, Akiko (21)—Arima Ineko

Aijima Kikuko (52), proprietress of Kotobuki-so mahjong parlor, Sugiyama's ex-wife and his girls' mother—Yamada Isuzu

Her husband, Aijima Sakae (54)—Nakamura Nobuo

Takeuchi Shigeko (46), Sugiyama's sister, owns a cosmetic products company—Sugimura Haruko

Kimura Kenji (20), Akiko's boyfriend—Taura Masami

Kawaguchi Noburo (27) ("Non-chan"), plays in a band, Kimura's friend—Takahashi Teiji

Kawaguchi's friends:

Tomita Saburō (33), bar tender at Gerbera—Suga Fujio

Matsushita Masatarō (24), student—Hasebe Tomoka

Maekawa Yasuko ("Yakko") (25)—Yamamoto Kazuko

Sekiguchi Tsumoru (56), Sugiyama's old friend—Yamamura Sō

Shimomura Yoshihira ("Gihei") (45), Chinchinken restaurant proprietor—Fujiwara Kamatari

His wife—Chichibu Haruko

Otsune (55), Komatsu saké bar proprietress—Urabe Kumeko

Customer at Komatsu—Tanaka Haruo

Ms. Tomizawa, Sugiyama's housekeeper—Nagaoka Teruko

Otafuko Restaurant proprietor—Shimamura Toshio

Gerbera Bar hostess—Sakura Mutsuko

Gerbera Bar customer—Masuda Junji

Mr. Sugai (58), Kawaguchi's mahjong friend—Sugawara Tsūsai

His shop apprentice who comes looking for him —Ishikawa Katsuji

Bank manager—Yamayoshi Kōsaku

Bank women employees:

Kawaguchi Nobu

Sora Nobuko

Eel restaurant waitress—Ikumi Aiko

Mahjong parlor customers:

Shirotani Kōji

Inoue Masahiko

Suenaga Isao

Etoile late night café customers:

Ishiyama Yūji

Sahara Yasushi

Shinoyama Masako

Takagi Nobuo

Nakamura Harue

Teraoka Kōji

Detective Wada (42), questioning Akiko at the Étoile café —Miyaguchi Seiji

A middle-aged man being questioned by police—Tanizaki Jun

Police station receptionist—Imai Kentarō

Dr. Kasahara (57), gynecologist—Miyoshi Eiko

Female patient at Kasahara Clinic—Miya Sachiko

Bar customers:

Niijima Tsutomu

Asami Hideo

Oni Shōsuke

Nurse at the town clinic—Chimura Yōko

1958

48. Color

Equinox Flower

彼岸花 *Higanbana*

Shōchiku

Story based on a novel by Satomi Ton, Script by Noda Kōgo and Ozu

Cinematography: Atsuta Yūharu

Music: Saitō Takanobu

Running time: 120 minutes

Number three on the *Kinema Jumpo* list

Old Music and New Realities

Ozu's bitter-sweet comedy, his first color film, wonderfully realized and beautifully shot, includes one of my favorite scenes in all his films.

Towards the last part of the film, we see the mother of the family, played by the great Tanaka Kinuyo, sitting in her living room and enjoying *nagauta* (a traditional way of singing, accompanied by shamisen, typical to the kabuki theater since the eighteenth century) being played on the radio. Her pleasure is evident by her face as her eyes sparkle and her neck and hands perform light, rhythmical movements to the music. We know that she is happy, because earlier we saw someone going to call her on the phone and tell her that her husband (played by Saburi Shin) finally agreed to the marriage of their daughter to the man she loves (typically of Ozu, we were not shown the actual phone conversation, but we can guess that it took place by the mother's good mood). Her happiness due to the good news is intensified by the pleasure she derives from the music. However, she is not aware (and we are yet to realize her unawareness) that her husband did not give his consent of his own free will but was tricked into doing so. Then, the grumpy Mr. Hirayama walks in and immediately turns off the radio. The happy wife suddenly realizes that something is wrong. After trying in vain to sooth his mood, she gives up on him and goes back to the radio and turns it on, wishing to resume her pleasure and to get rid of the bitter taste of his grumpiness (and perhaps also secretly celebrate the triumph over his stubbornness). But the husband shouts at her to turn the radio off, demonstrating again his egotism and bad temper. She does as she's told, while fixing him with a defiant stare. In fact, the husband's triumph over the radio only emphasizes how pathetic he has become; this is the only time in the whole film that his wish is triumphant. In all other matters except the radio, he is defeated by his womenfolk: he agrees to the marriage against his wishes, he gives in and says he'll attend the wedding after declaring it will take place without his presence, and in the last scene he agrees to go visit his daughter and make peace in spite of himself.

There is another striking case of the use of traditional music in the film. In one of the last scenes, the husband meets his old friends for a class reunion. One of the friends (played by Ryū Chishū) is urged by the others to sing a traditional song. At first, he refuses, saying that there is no longer a place for this old stuff in contemporary times, but eventually relents. He sings an old epic poem, typical of the pre-war period, about the loyalty of a son to his father and about giving one's life when at war. After singing a few verses, he stops and refuses to go on. The classmates then start singing a popular song from their school days on the same theme. In the very last scene, the father is seen on the train, going to meet his daughter, and quietly singing to himself the same old song. Times have changed, he has to admit, but it is still not easy for him to give up his traditional values. In many ways, he is still a man of the past. A little earlier, his friend told him that he had made peace with his own daughter, who had eloped with her boyfriend (Hirayama's earlier attempt to bring about reconciliation between father and daughter was another of his many failures in this film; still, even when he realized the danger of alienation between father and daughter, he did not recognize the danger for himself, and refused to allow his daughter to be married, only because she chose the man without asking him first). It is better to admit defeat of the old generation, Ozu seems to say, and keep the family together in spite of everything, hinting, perhaps, also to Japan's defeat in the war and the need to go along with modern sensibilities (including the making of color films . . .). It is interesting to note here also that in an earlier conversation the wife said that she was happiest during the war, in spite of all the hardships, because then the whole family was together; the husband, as usual, disagrees, but perhaps he learns better.

The film opens with a scene at a railway station, with attendants talking about the many newlywed couples boarding trains. This is followed by a wedding scene, in which Hirayama gives a speech, praising the new idea of love-marriages, and then goes on to contradict himself when it comes to his own daughter. The film ends on the train, with the father going to meet his daughter for a final reconciliation. Another director would have shown us the meeting (or the wedding, or both), and squeeze out some more emotion and tears from the scene. But Ozu has already told us—or rather, shown us—everything he had to tell and show, sending us home with a little smile on our face, and perhaps a little tear in our eye.

Cast:

Actors and characters—thirty-six in all—are matched on the film's opening credits, but in a different order than the one offered below.

Characters' age is given according to the script, and some further identifying details are added.

Hirayama Wataru (55), company executive—Saburi Shin

His wife, Kiyoko (48)—Tanaka Kinuyo

Their elder daughter, Setsuko (23)—Arima Ineko

Their younger daughter, Hisako (17)—Kuwano Miyuki

Taniguchi Masahiko (32), Setsuko's fiancé, a company employee—Sada Keiji

Mikami Shūkichi (56), Hirayama's old friend—Ryū Chishū

His daughter, Mikami Tomoko (24), bar hostess —Kuga Yoshiko

Her boyfriend, Naganuma Ichirō (28), musician —Watanabe Fumio

Hirayama's other old friends:

Kawai Toshihiko (55), whose daughter's wedding reception the Hirayamas attend—Nakamura Nobuo

Horie Heinosuke (56)—Kita Ryūji

Sasaki Hatsu (52), Kyoto traditional inn owner—Naniwa Chieko

Her daughter, Yukiko (26)—Yamamoto Fujiko

Omatsu, Sasaki's inn maid—Tachibana Kazue

Hirayama's co-worker, Soga Ryōzō (seen once in his office) —Toake Hisao

Kondo Shōtarō (28), Hirayama's submissive employee —Takahashi Teiji

Company worker A (sitting next to Kondo)—Oni Shōsuke

Office girl, showing in guests into Hirayama's office —Sora Nobuko

Wakamatsu Restaurant proprietress—Takahashi Toyo

Hirayama's housekeeper, Ms. Tomisawa—Nagaoka Teruko

Luna Bar hostess, Akemi—Sakura Mutsuko

Barman in Luna—Suenaga Isao

Waitress in Luna—Mine Hisako

Men in class reunion:

Nakanishi (white hair)—Egawa Ureo

Sugai (the man with seven daughters)—Sugawara Tsūsai

Hayashi (seventh man at the table)—Takeda Norikazu

A (leaves the room)—Kobayashi Tokuji

Hospital nurse—Chimura Yōko

Tokyo inn maid—Ikumi Aiko

Gamagori inn maid—Sasaki Tsuneko

At the wedding reception:

Toastmaster—Kawamura Kōhei

Singing guest—Hasegawa Gazan

The bride—Kiyokawa Akiko

The bridegroom—Kawakane Masanao

Train station workers at the beginning of the film:

A—Imai Kentarō

B—Inoue Masahiko

Train conductor (on the train to Hiroshima)—Suga Fujio

1959

49. Color

Good Morning

お早よう *Ohayō*

Shōchiku

Script by Noda Kōgo and Ozu

Cinematography: Atsuta Yūharu

Music: Mayuzumi Toshirō

Running time: 94 minutes

What Does a "Good Morning" Actually Signify?

A major theme in this film is lifted and recast from *I was Born, But . . .* , which is the conflict between the two young boys and the unfathomable world of adults. While in the earlier film the stumbling block was power, this time it is manners, although the trigger to the conflict is the parents' refusal to buy a television set (in the previous film it was the children seeing their father making a fool of himself in a home movie). When told that they talk too much the children point out the non-stop niceties uttered by the grown-ups such as "good morning," "it's a fine weather," and so on, which to their ears sound totally redundant, although we are told that these exchanges are necessary for maintaining civil society. Rather than a (short) hunger strike, this time round the children go on a longer silence strike: You are telling us to shut up? OK, we will, indefinitely, at home and in school. The conflict is solved only with the purchase of the coveted television set, although the parents' stated motivation is to help the unemployed neighbor who found a job selling appliances door to door (actually, the mother would have much preferred a washing machine).

Apart from this main story line, other scenes are recognizable from previous films, although there are new themes as well. Comic situations are created along several lines. One is the silence strike that causes misunderstanding when the boys fail to answer the next-door neighbor's "good morning" and the neighborhood's housewives naturally put the blame on their mother, leading to a comedy of errors. Another is the farting game in which the boys engage, with unpleasant consequences for one of them. In a way, the farting is also a kind of empty communication, as the film makes clear in various ways (and what we hear is not actual farting, but whistling sounds at various pitches). Again, in a farcical scene the boys try to make themselves understood using pantomime, but the adults completely fail to understand their simple message. And there is more comedy, often on the verge between the nonsensical and the painful.

Ozu uses here one of his most elaborate sets and keeps experimenting within his familiar style. We first view the houses in this small project from the back, with the familiar Ozuian shots of loaded washing lines. Later we enter each house, sometimes from the front and other times through the side doors. We look into rooms in the opposite house through open windows and doors. We see people moving to and fro along the raised embankment at the back of the houses. All these movements and connecting shots are masterfully orchestrated. The time frame is also tightly controlled; according to the script, the film covers one week, as follows:

> Tuesday: Most characters are introduced; the children request a television set.
>
> Wednesday: The children are scolded, go on a silence strike.
>
> Thursday: The children don't answer the neighbor's greeting, causing a misunderstanding. In the evening they fail to explain by pantomime that they should take lunch money to school.
>
> [Friday: Not shown; the children would have gone to school without bringing the money.]
>
> Saturday: The children still won't talk.
>
> Sunday: The teacher visits, and the children go missing, later found. The parents buy a television set and the conflict is solved.
>
> Finally, Monday: The children answer the neighbor's greeting, causing another misunderstanding.

On the Tuesday, Wednesday, Thursday, and Monday, the narration starts in the morning, on Saturday in the evening, and on Sunday in the afternoon.

So, do the children have a fair point in their protest against the adults' niceties? Kayoko tells her younger brother that because of the obligatory use of polite expressions, he fails to tell Setsuko that he likes her. And indeed, as the film concludes, the two are seen waiting for the train while exchanging observations on the weather.

People seem to remember this film for the farting, which may have damaged its reputation, but in fact it is a complex comedy, full of interest, beautifully and elaborately shot.

Cast:

The opening credits list the names of twenty-six actors, all matched with their characters. They are given below in a different order, with characters' age and some further identifying details added according to the script.

The housing project in the film has eight houses in two rows of four, and we get to know the families living in five of them:

Hayashi

Keitarō (46), company employee—Ryū Chishū

His wife, Tamiko (37)—Miyake Kuniko

Their elder son, Minoru (13)—Shitara Kōji

Their younger son, Isamu (7)—Shimazu Masahiko

Arita Setsuko (24), Tamiko's sister, company employee —Kuga Yoshiko

Tomizawa (on Hayashi's right side)

Hiroshi, retired and looking for a job, often drunk —Tōno Eijirō

His wife (48), Toyoko—Nagaoka Teruko

Maruyama (on Hayashi's left side), they move out later

Akira (30), musician, the only owner of a television set —Ōizumi Akira

His wife Midori (25), works in a cabaret—Izumi Kyōko

Ōkubo (across from Maruyama)

Zennosuke (49)—Takeda Norikazu

His wife, Shige (40)—Takahashi Toyo

Their son, Zenichi (13)—Fujiki Masuo

Haraguchi (across from Hayashi)

Tatsuzō (42)—Tanaka Haruo

His wife, Kikue (38)—Sugimura Haruko

Their son, Kōzō (13)—Shirota Hajime

Kikue's mother, Mitsue (62), a midwife—Miyoshi Eiko

Outside the housing project or visiting it:

Fukui Heiichirō (29), unemployed, translates and teaches English at home—Sada Keiji

His older sister, Fukui Kayoko (39), an automobile salesperson—Sawamura Sadako

Mr. Itō (35), Minoru's homeroom teacher—Suga Fujio

Ms. Sakuma (32), Isamu's homeroom teacher—Chimura Yōko

A pushy vendor (45-46)—Tonoyama Taiji

His accomplice (33), selling alarm bells—Satake Akio

Policeman—Morozumi Keijirō

Ukiyo *oden* restaurant proprietor—Shimamura Toshio

His wife—Sakura Mutsuko

Customer—Sugawara Tsūsai

*

50. Color

Floating Weeds

浮草 *Ukigusa*

Daiei

Script by Noda Kōgo and Ozu

Cinematography: Miyagawa Kazuo

Music: Saitō Takanobu

Running time: 119 minutes

The Weeds Are Still Floating

This one is Ozu's nearest remake of one of his earlier films, following closely the plot of *Story of Floating Weeds* from 1934, although with some changes and additions. It is also one of his most beautiful visually, but for some reason, it did not gain the attention it deserves, certainly not at the time of its release. Perhaps it seemed outmoded. Although it takes place in the present (1959) it may as well be happening at the time of the original film (1934). There are no modern facilities in the old town visited by the actors' troop, not a television set in sight, and the troop's act is extremely old-fashioned.

A memorable scene repeated and enhanced in this version is of the fight between the troop's head Komajurō and his mistress and leading actress Sumiko while the rain is pouring down. The two are trapped under roofs on opposite sides of the street, walking to and fro like a caged lion and lioness, the heavily falling rain separating them and curbing their violence, as they keep hurling abuses and complaints at each other. The scene is masterfully dialogued and played, but perhaps it is memorable also because rain is so rare in Ozu's films.

In the former version, the troop arrived by train and at night; this time they arrive by boat and by day. The troop is larger this time, and there are more interactions with the town people, which allows for various comical scenes. The cast includes three very substantial new faces. Nakamura Ganjirō was in fact a kabuki actor before he started to appear in films around the time this one was made. Perhaps out of respect for his art, he is not actually shown on stage among his mediocre colleagues. He will be cast once again in *The End of Summer*. Regrettably, the two leading ladies appear only in this one Ozu film. Kyō Machiko became world-famous to a certain degree after acting as the samurai's wife in Kurosawa Akira's *Rashomon*. She had a very long and distinguished career, appearing in films by all Japanese major directors of the 1950's and 60's (and one Hollywood film, *The Teahouse of the August Moon*). Wakao Ayako, although ten years younger than Kyō, was also one of the biggest stars of the same period. There is only one actor who was in both this and the previous version: Mitsui Kōji, who played the adolescent son then, and here plays the actor Kichinosuke.

Cast:

There are thirty-nine names of actors on the opening credits, but they are *not* matched with their characters, and some have not been identified yet. The age of characters is given according to the script, and some descriptions added.

The actors' troop:

Arashi Komajurō (58)—Nakamura Ganjirō

Sumiko (34), the leading actress and Komajurō's mistress —Kyō Machiko

Kayo (23), the younger actress—Wakao Ayako

The three leading actors, often seen together:

Kichinosuke (37)—Mitsui Kōji

Sentarō (34)—Ushio Mantarō

Yatazō (47)—Tanaka Haruo

Senshō (65)—Date Tadashi

His grandson, Masao (6)—Shimazu Masahiko

Rokusaburō (58)—Hanabu Tatsuo

Shige (52), plays the shamisen—Urabe Kumeko

Kamenosuke (30), plays the clarinet—Nakata Tsutomu

Shōkichi (nicknamed "Tokoyama") (32)—Marui Tarō

Sugiyama (nicknamed "Bungeibu") (25)—Irie Yōsuke

Chōtarō (43)—Fujimura Yoshiaki

Kimura (45), the agent who disappeared—Hoshi Hikaru

The town:

Honma Oyoshi (45), Tsuruya restaurant proprietress —Sugimura Haruko

Her son, Kiyoshi (21)—Kawaguchi Hiroshi

Aioi Theater owner (57)—Ryū Chishū

Tokuzō, theater usher

Ogawa barbershop:

Aiko (22)—Nozoe Hitomi

Her mother—Takahashi Toyo

Her father—Miyajima Kenichi

Customer—Minakata Nobuo

Umetaya shop/brothel:

Okatsu (26)—Sakura Mutsuko

Yae (28)—Kahara Natsuko

Customer—Sasaki Masatoki

Antique dealer—Sugawara Tsūsai

Sailor—Misumi Hachirō

Dock attendent—Sugita Kō

Men waiting for the boat:

Sakai Saburō

Maruyama Osamu

Murozumi, post office worker—Shiho Kyōsuke

Joe Ohara

Hida Kisao

Takeuchi Tetsurō

Yamaguchi Ken

Sugimori Rin

Matsumura Wakashiro

Takesato Mitsuko

Shingū Nobuko

1960

51. Color

Late Autumn

秋日和 *Akibiyori* (Literally: "A fine autumn day")

Shōchiku

Story based on a novel by Satomi Ton, Script by Noda Kōgo and Ozu

Cinematography: Atsuta Yūharu

Music: Saitō Takanobu

Running time: 129 minutes

Number five on the *Kinema Jumpo* list

Always a Fine Day

The Japanese title of this film means "a fine autumn day," and indeed, most of Ozu's films take place during fine days in autumn, or hot and clear days in summer. So much so, that one would hear complaints that this trait makes Ozu's films unrealistic; after all, there are relatively few such lovely days each year in Japan, contrary to the impression Ozu's films might leave on the unaware viewer. There *is* the rare shower in Ozu's films; for example, the memorable scene of the fight between the actor and his mistress in *Story of Floating Weeds*, repeated in *Floating Weeds*, which takes place in a downpour (although the characters hardly get wet, being sheltered under the cover of roofs on both sides of the street; the rain serves as a kind of barrier, curbing their violence). *Tokyo Twilight* takes place in the cold of winter, adding to the gloom of the melodramatic story. But these are relatively rare examples.

Some directors love to film in foul weather. Kurosawa Akira's characters often had to struggle with the elements, drenched in rain and covered in mud (it is said that when John Ford met Kurosawa he said tersely: "You like rain"). But does this make Kurosawa's films more realistic? Ozu's realism is in the human condition, which is often harsh, or at least sad. When life is so difficult, at least let's have some fine weather, Ozu seems to say.

This film is a kind of remake of *Late Spring*, made eleven years earlier. In the earlier film, a daughter living with a widowed father is talked into agreeing to a marriage, although she likes her life with her father just fine. In *Late Autumn*, the daughter lives with a widowed mother, but the situation is the same. In both films the daughter has to be tricked into believing her parent wishes to remarry in order for her to agree to leave home and start a family of her own. In both cases, the parent remains alone.

There are also several differences between the two films. In *Late Spring* focus was on the beauty of Japanese culture—a Nō play, a ceramic vase, Kyoto's temples—a motif somewhat emphasized also in Ozu's next film, *The Munekata Sisters*, and occasionally reappearing in later films as well, although not with the same insistence. The comedy is there but is subdued. In this film, on the other hand, the comic elements are up front, often taking the edge off the more serious ones. The "old boys" are almost cruel in their search for fun, ignoring the damage they might inflict on other people's lives. They are kept in place by a young, sensible girl, Yuriko (the lovely and spirited Okada Mariko), but she, too, is out to have fun. And as he often does, Ozu offers a little inside joke when the actor Saburi Shin is late for the memorial service in the beginning of the film, as he was years earlier in *The Brothers and Sisters of the Toda Family*.

There is also a difference in the ending of the two films. The father who marries off his daughter in *Late Spring*, as well as the one in *An Autumn Afternoon*, Ozu's last film, although they both insisted that their daughter get married, seem almost shattered once the wedding takes place. The father in the earlier film looks sad and forlorn in the last scene, sitting at home alone, peeling a fruit, while the one in the later film (both played by Ryū Chishū) gets unpleasantly drunk and complains loudly of his loneliness. The mother in this film, on the other hand, although left alone too, seems far less distressed, even smiling a little knowing smile to herself, reminding us perhaps of Noriko's knowing, accepting smile towards the end of *Tokyo Story* (both roles played by Hara Setsuko): that's how life is, and there is no use complaining about it. Yes, tomorrow will be a sadder, lonelier day, but it might also be another fine autumn day, one of those days that make life less unbearable.

Cast:

There are thirty-six names of actors on the opening credits, but they are *not* matched with their characters, and some have not been identified yet. The age of characters is given according to the script.

The mother, Miwa Akiko (45)—Hara Setsuko

Her daughter, Ayako (24)—Tsukasa Yōko

Her brother-in-law, Miwa Shūkichi (59)—Ryū Chishū

Ayako's marriage prospect, Gotō Shōtarō (31)—Sada Keiji

Family friend Mamiya Sōichi (54)—Saburi Shin

His wife, Fumiko (42)—Sawamura Sadako

His daughter, Michiko (18)—Kuwano Miyuki

His son, Tadao (7)—Shimazu Masahiko

Family friend Taguchi Shūzō (54)—Nakamura Nobuo

His wife, Nobuko (46)—Miyake Kuniko

His married daughter, Hidaka Yōko (24)—Tashiro Yuriko

His son, Kazuo (18)—Shitara Kōji

Family friend Hirayama Seiichirō (53)—Kita Ryūji

His son, Kōichi (21)—Mikami Shinichirō

Ayako's friend, Sasaki Yuriko (25)—Okada Mariko

Her father, Yoshitarō (52)—Takeda Norikazu

Her stepmother, Hisa (46)—Sakura Mutsuko

Akiko's employer, Kuwata Sakae (45)—Minami Yoshie

Her husband, Kuwata Shūkichi (56)—Toake Hisao

Ayako's coworkers:

Sugiyama Tsuneo (31), Gotō's friend—Watanabe Fumio

Getting married:

Takamatsu Shigeko (25)—Chino Kakuko

Hattori Susumu (32)—Hasebe Tomoka

Wakamatsu Restaurant proprietress (50)—Takahashi Toyo

Sushi bar customer—Sugawara Tsūsai

Man in memorial service, remembers the late Miwa—Suga Fujio

Receptionist, showing guests into Mamiya's office—Iwashita Shima

Eel restaurant waitress—Ikumi Aiko

Barman in Luna—Suenaga Isao

Hirayama's house help, Ms. Tomizawa (45)—Yamamoto Tami

Shirotani Kōji

Yamashina Yukari

Mitsukawa Kyōko

Hara Yoshiko

Kawamura Kōhei

Oni Shōsuke

Inagawa Zenichi

Characters with speaking lines include: priests in the memorial service, Ayako's coworkers, golf store clerk, etc.

1961

52. Color

The End of Summer

小早川家の秋 *Kohayakawake no aki* (Literally: "The autumn of Kohayakawa family")

Takarazuka Eiga/Tōhō
Script by Noda Kōgo and Ozu
Cinematography: Nakai Asakazu
Music: Mayuzumi Toshirō
Running time: 103 minutes

On Brightness and Darkness

This is one of Ozu's most beautiful color films, with constant shifts between bright and dark scenes. The brightness and darkness are not used as symbols; the cremation of the old man's body takes place under dazzling light, while some of the most comic scenes take place in relative darkness. This is another of the many ways by which Ozu surprises his audience, acting contrary to their expectations. In fact, this is also another expression of Ozu's realism; in real life, terrible things often happen under the sun's naked light rather than under the cover of darkness.

The story is a combination of familiar themes: the death of a parent, the need to marry off a daughter, the breaking up of a large family. But as always with Ozu, there are some new twists and turns, and some new ways of telling which we encounter as we become familiar with the Kohayakawa family, the owners of a small saké brewery in a Kyoto suburb, and with the lives and fortunes of its numerous members.

The history of the family—as their chief clerk admits—is very complicated, and not all the details are clear. The printed script yields the following information:

The current head of the family, Manbei, who was an orphan, married the eldest daughter (name unknown) of the Kohayakawa family, and was adopted into it, becoming the head of the family following his father-in-law. Manbei's deceased wife had two sisters:

The elder, Shige, married into the Kato family from Nagoya; she appears when Manbei first has his heart attack, and also at the cremation.

The younger, Teruko, is seen several times with her husband, Kitagawa Yanosuke, "the uncle from Osaka" who is trying to get Akiko married to his friend.

Manbei also has a real brother, Hayashi Seizō, who comes from Tokyo when Manbei has his heart attack but does not attend the cremation (what we see near the end of the film is not the formal funeral, which would take place a few days later).

Manbei had at least three children:

The elder son, Kōichi, did not want to continue in the family business and became a university professor. He married Akiko, who now works in an art gallery, and had a son, Minoru, but died young.

The elder daughter, Fumiko, married Hisao, who apparently was also adopted into the family and runs the business. They have one son, Masao.

The youngest daughter, Noriko, who works in the office of a large company, is yet to be married.

Manbei may also have had a daughter, Yuriko, with his former mistress Tsune, but the true identity of Yuriko's father is not clear.

As often with Ozu films, the story is a constant play between the older and younger generations. The focus may be on old Manbei and his shenanigans, but it is also about the marriage of the younger daughter, as well as the possible marriage of the widowed daughter-in-law. Somehow, in spite of the large and complex family, everything seems simpler and more concise than in some of the other films (and with a running time of only 103 minutes, this film is considerably shorter than most of Ozu's other post-war films). Also, some emotions and intentions are more starkly exposed than usual: the lust for life of the old man, the gold-digging of the mother and daughter from Kyoto, and even the deep affection between sisters-in-law, played by Hara Setsuko and Tsukasa Yōko, who played mother and daughter in a similar situation in Ozu's former film. This affection is expressed through the careful use of one of Ozu's well-known means of telling-through-showing: the action in unison. We see the two women squat and rise as one, as a sign for their deep mutual understanding and same-mindedness.

The End of Summer is one of only three films that Ozu made for companies other than his home studio, Shōchiku. This one was made for Tōhō, using that studio's staff rather than the usual people who worked with Ozu in most of his post-war films (and in some cases, also pre-war ones). Perhaps this also explains the appearance of many unfamiliar faces among the cast. Only four of Ozu's regulars appear here (Hara Setsuko, Sugimura Haruko, Ryū Chishū, and Katō Daisuke, a semi-regular), as well as a few actors who appeared in only one other film (Nakamura Ganjirō, Tsukasa Yōko, Naniwa Chieko, Mochizuki Yūko), but many appear only in this film, and must have come from Tōhō's stables. Some of these one-timers give a truly wonderful performance: emotional but confident (Aratama Michiyo as the elder daughter Fumiko), slightly comical (Sazanka Kyū as the chief clerk), or farcical (Morishige Hisaya as Akiko's hapless suitor).

According to Donald Richie,[11] in this film, Ozu went a long way to accommodate actors' wishes: Mochizuki Yūko, a famous actress who earlier had a short scene in only one of Ozu's film, wanted to be in another, and Ozu's regular actor Ryū Chishū also had to be fitted in somehow, so Ozu added the scene of the farmer husband and wife commenting on the cycle of life towards the end of the film, a scene that many critics have found superfluous. And on a lighter note, this is almost the only Ozu film with the participation of *gaijin* or foreigners (there was a German man in one scene of *The Lady and the Beard*), in the figures of "George" and "Harry," Yuriko's boyfriends; their real identity is unknown, and they get no mention in the credits.

The film ends on a somber note, with crows perching on tombstones, but we must remember that earlier we heard that Noriko is going to marry the man she loves, and a new life begins for her. Akiko also has her choice of going on living as she pleases. While everything has ended for the old man, not all is dark.

11. Richie, *Ozu*, 63.

Cast:

There are thirty-eight names of actors and actresses on the film's opening credits, but they are *not* matched with their characters, and some have not been identified yet. There are many actors appearing for the first and only time, because the film was made for Tōhō, using that studio's staff. Age of characters is given according to the script.

The father, Kohayakawa Manbei (65)—Nakamura Ganjirō

The widow of Manbei's elder son (Kōichi), Akiko (37)
—Hara Setsuko

Akiko's son, Minoru (13)—Hayakawa Kyōji

Manbei's daughter, Fumiko (32)—Aratama Michiyo

Her husband, Hisao (36)—Kobayashi Keiju

Her son, Masao—Shimazu Masahiko

Manbei's youngest daughter, Noriko (24)—Tsukasa Yōko

Manbei's old mistress, Sasaki Tsune (48)—Naniwa Chieko

Her daughter, Yuriko (21)—Dan Reiko

Noriko's office coworker, Nakanishi Takako (24)—Shirakawa Yumi

Noriko's chosen partner (goes to Sapporo), Teramoto Tadashi (29)
—Takarada Akira

Manbei's real brother, from Tokyo, Hayashi Seizō (54)
—Endo Tatsuo

Manbei's sister from Nagoya, Kato Shige (48)—Sugimura Haruko

Manbei's brother-in-law, "uncle from Osaka," Kitagawa Yanosuke (45)—Katō Daisuke

His wife, Teruko (38)—Tōgō Haruko

Chief clerk, Yamaguchi Nobuhisa (42)—Sazanka Kyū

Clerk, Maruyama Rokutarō (28)—Fujiki Yū

Akiko's suitor, Isomura Eiichirō (48)—Morishige Hisaya

Akemi, hostess at "Lila Bar" (26)—Tamaki Miseyo

Doctor—Uchida Asao

Farmer (57)—Ryū Chishū
Farmer's wife (48)—Mochizuki Yūko

Takatori Makiko
Higashi Mayumi
Yoshikawa Masae
Yūki Michiyo
Nishikawa Tomiko
Tachibana Mitsuko
Kawahara Ken
Shimizu Yoshikazu
Watanabe Hideto
Umeka Fumiko
Tsugawa Akemi
Mori Akiko
Chimura Katsuko
Sono Yukari
Yamamoto Mikiko
Segawa Kyōsuke

All the above-listed actors without identified characters appeared only in this one Ozu film. Unidentified characters include young men and women at the farewell party, two office girls in the family's business, people in a bar including the dancing hostess and customer, etc. Also unaccounted for are the two foreigners playing "George" and "Harry."

1962

53. Color
An Autumn Afternoon
秋刀魚の味 *Sanma no aji* (Literally: "The taste of *sanma* [a fish eaten in autumn]")

Shōchiku
Script by Noda Kōgo and Ozu
Cinematography: Atsuta Yūharu
Music: Saitō Takanobu
Running time: 113 minutes
Number eight on the *Kinema Jumpo* list

Ozu's Private "Family"

An Autumn Afternoon turned out to be Ozu's last film. He was working on his next project when a particularly virulent form of cancer ended his life in great pain while professionally he was still in peak form. Everything that was wonderful in his earlier films can be found in this final one, including the marvelous cast of familiar actors and actresses.

Much has already been written about Ozu's regular cast, which gives viewers the feeling of meeting with familiar family members. In some cases the family relations were real; the beautiful and vivacious Okada Mariko, who plays the daughter-in-law Akiko in this film (and who played Yuriko in *Late Autumn*), was the daughter of Okada Tokihiku, a star of Ozu's silent films who died at the young age of thirty, only one year after the birth of his daughter. This daughter herself became a distinguished actress, and learned from Ozu about the father she never got to know. There are a few other such cases, but the main point is that through participating in his films, actors and actresses became "relatives," parts of a large and loyal family, which also included the behind-the-scenes staff.

What happened to "Ozu's family" after the death of their *sensei* and "father"? Most famous is the fate of Hara Setsuko, who is not in this final film, but who had major roles in six earlier ones. She retired from the screen shortly after Ozu's death, and was never seen in public again, leading an even more stubbornly private life than Greta Garbo. Her appeal is still strong, apparently; in its issue of March 2011, the magazine *Shinko* published eight pieces by writers and actors on "rediscovering Hara Setsuko," and included a DVD of one of her earliest films, *Inochi no kanmuri* (*The Crown of Life*, a surprisingly socially oriented 1936 silent film by director Uchida Tomu, in which Hara had a minor part).

However, unlike Hara, most other Ozu regulars continued on with successful careers. I was struck by the fact—was it a coincidence or an intended tribute?—that several of Ozu regulars appeared years later in the films of another gifted director, Itami Jūzō, who died tragically in 1997, aged sixty-four. In Itami's first film, *The Funeral* (1984), Ryū Chishū, Ozu's most regular actor, plays the wonderful part of a Buddhist abbot; in fact, Ryū was familiar with the part not only because he was the son of a Buddhis priest, but because he had played a similar role in director Yamada Yōji's popular series of films *It's Hard Being a Man* (known as "Tora-san films," after their hero, and reputed to have been influenced by Ozu's *Kihachi mono* and some other films), which was the longest in film history at the time (and is still the longest series made by the same director) with forty-eight installments. Ryū was in most of them (as well as in hundreds of other Japanese films), and is probably remembered better by the Japanese public for that role than for his roles in Ozu's films. He turned up again in Itami's fourth film, *A Taxing Woman's Return* (1988) as a retired Buddhist priest. He was eighty-four years old at the time, and still had several films ahead of him, including an impressive part in Kurosawa Akira's 1990 film *Dreams*. The above-mentioned Okada Mariko also appeared in two of Itami's films; in his second one, *Tampopo* (1985), she had a small role as a refined lady who teaches a group of debutants how to eat spaghetti politely, until her intentions are frustrated by a rude foreigner, and in the third,

A Taxing Woman (1987), she played another refined lady, the wife of the corrupt businessman under investigation. What a pleasure it is to recognize her as the fiery young woman of Ozu's films. And finally, also in *Tampopo,* in the minor role of the "professor" who turns out to be not as naïve as the con-man who was laying a trap for him was thinking, it is possible to identify none other than Nakamura Nobuo, a veteran of Ozu's cast since *Tokyo Story* (the son-in-law), and who also appears in *An Autumn Afternoon* as the classmate who holds a grudge against their old teacher.

These actors and many others appeared also in the 1983 tribute film to Ozu, directed and scripted by Inoue Kazuo, which in the original Japanese had the meaningful title *Ikite wa mite keredo* ("I lived, but . . . "), but in English has the uninspiring title *The Life and Works of Yasujiro Ozu* (at least in the IMDb website's listing). In this film—which is highly recommended to all Ozu lovers—relatives and friends of Ozu, as well as film directors and actors, talk about his life and work from various angles. Ryū Chishū, Nakamura Nobuo, Okada Mariko, Sugimura Haruko and several other actors participated, but Hara Setsuko refused to immerge from seclusion even for a cause such as this. Perhaps the most moving moment in this film is when Kishida Kyōko (who plays the bar hostess in *An Autumn Afternoon*, her only appearance in an Ozu film which made her a "last minute" member of the "family") reads Ozu's poem on bringing his mother's ashes for burial on Mount Kōya.

These are some of the many aspects that link *An Autumn Afternoon* to the cinematic and the real worlds. The film itself brings together several of Ozu's recurring themes; not only family break-ups and the marrying off of a daughter, but also social issues relating to the lives of the *salaryman*, which go back to the films of the 1930's and early 1950's. The humor is there, and the beauty and poignancy—everything we are looking for in an Ozu film.

Cast:

There are twenty-six names of actors and actresses on the film's opening credits, but they are *not* matched with their characters, and a few have not been matched with their roles yet.

Hirayama Shūhei (57)—Ryū Chishū

His elder son, Kōichi (32)—Sada Keiji

His wife, Akiko (28)—Okada Mariko

His daughter, Michiko (24)—Iwashita Shima

His younger son, Kazuo (21)—Mikami Shinichirō

Hirayama's old friend and Michiko's boss, Kawai Shūzō (57) —Nakamura Nobuo

His wife, Nobuko (46)—Miyake Kuniko

Horie Shin, Hirayama's old friend (57)—Kita Ryūji

His young second wife, Tamako (28)—Tamaki Miseyo

Sakuma Seitarō (72), the old teacher nicknamed "the Gourd" —Tōno Eijirō

His daughter, Tomoko (48)—Sugimura Haruko

Participants in class reunion:

Sugai—Sugawara Tsūsai

Watanabe—Oda Masao

Nakanishi—Ogata Yasuo

Miura Yutaka, Kōichi's colleague and love interest of Michiko (26) —Yoshida Teruo

Sakamoto Yoshitarō (48), mechanic, Hirayama's former subordinate—Katō Daisuke

Proprietress ("Madam") of Tory's Bar (32)—Kishida Kyōko

Wakamatsu Restaurant proprietress—Takahashi Toyo

Sasaki Yōko (32), Hirayama's office woman—Asaji Shinobu

Taguchi Fusako (24), Hirayama's employee who is getting married —Maki Noriko

Akiko's neighbor, Ogawa Sayako (33)—Shiga Matsuko

Tory's Bar customers:

A—Suga Fujio

B—Inagawa Zenichi

Bride's kimono salon—Yamamoto Tami

Komachi Kushiro

Imai Kentarō

***

Epilogue: Watching Ozu

I can still clearly remember the first time I watched *Tokyo Story* and *Equinox Flower* in the Jerusalem Cinematheque decades ago, and the feeling I was left with when the lights were turned back on: "I can't quite articulate it yet, but I just watched something special." I desired to see more, but during the 1980's Ozu's films were not so readily available, and opportunities to watch them were few and far between.

In 1989 I went to study in Japan on a scholarship, and on visiting the university library, discovered that I could watch films on VHS tapes or laser discs. On telling the student working there that I wanted to watch whichever Ozu films they had in store, the guy was visibly shocked: Really?! Ozu?? It is still not quite clear to me if he was shocked on account of me being a foreigner interested in Ozu, or more likely: why would anyone want to watch such old stuff?

In the following years, I was able to acquire some VHS tapes as well as books on Ozu, and started to feel the urge to write about his cinema, and in particular to identify the actors that kept appearing in different films. It was a project I started, stopped and restarted several times, reviving it occasionally between some more urgent obligations. It took nearly 35 years to bring it to fruition, but I can feel a certain satisfaction for not having given it up.

Before leaving Japan, I went on a pilgrimage to Ozu's grave in Kamakura and met with Donald Richie in Tokyo, telling him of my project and receiving his blessing. At the time it didn't occur to me that it would be such a long time before I realized my intention, and by now, sadly, Richie is long gone.

A decade after leaving, I returned to live in Japan once again, and restarted my effort to collect information on Ozu's films, a task which became gradually easier with the advance of the Internet. Occasionally, there were some special opportunities to watch a film or gather information. I remember an exhibition of Ozu memorabilia held at the Daimaru Department Store, where a few films were also screened. I sat through one of them, aware that I was the only foreigner and by far the youngest person in the audience, and feeling satisfied when I laughed when everyone else was laughing, and perhaps also shed a tear at the same time.

Not long after returning to Japan I happened to teach a class at a renowned women's college. The class was open to the college's alumnae, so the range of ages was between about twenty to fifty. This time it was I who was feeling shocked when it turned out that not one of those well-educated women was aware of Ozu's films.

A few years ago, I happened to be in Paris in time for a Japanese cultural festival. Luckily, a retrospective of ten Ozu films was showing just when I was there. This was a good opportunity to watch some digitally restored films in a cinema hall, while in Japan, ironically, chances to do so are rare. What amazed me the most was the attendance at the screenings. Films were screened five times a day for two weeks, and whenever I went, there was a long line of people waiting patiently outside to be admitted into the small cinema near the *Sorbonne*, which had about 120 seats, almost all of which were taken on the three screenings I attended. So, kudos to the French who still appreciate high culture in all its forms. It's still hard to describe my feelings at the time; elation comes close.

Back in Japan and back to watching old DVDs, but by now the films are also available on the Internet, some for free, others for a fee. The computer screen is not the best medium for watching Ozu's beautiful creations, but this availability allowed me to finally complete my project, although it can never be fully completed. It remains to be seen whether anybody else is interested.

Now, Where Did I Also See . . . ?

One of my main purposes in writing this book was to identify the actors who reappear in various Ozu films, and for that purpose the included actors' list was created, but there are also repeated themes, names, scenes etc. Some have already been pointed out in the earlier film descriptions, and following are some more (to save space, the numbers of the films on the attached list are given rather than the titles).

Deathbed scenes

The dying person speaks (35, 46, 47).

The dying person doesn't speak, or is already dead (25, 27, 37, 45, 52).

Dying out of bed (42).

A critically ill child

Sometimes the illness is due to overindulging on sweets, and in many cases the parent or someone close is driven to drastic means to get the money needed for the child's treatment, including robbery or prostitution (16, 22, 29, 33, 35, 40).

Slapping and beating

In most cases when a person is being slapped on the face once or even repeatedly, they take it stoically.

A man spanks or slaps a boy (24, 29).

A man restrains a boy physically (43, 49).

A man slaps a woman once (36).

A man slaps a woman repeatedly (27, 40, 42).

A man slaps a man repeatedly (25).

A man slaps and beats two women and a young man (31, 50).

A boy slaps a man repeatedly (29).

A woman slaps a man repeatedly (46, 47).

Kisses

Kisses are extremely rare, perhaps due to Ozu's shyness, but also due to pre-war censorship which forbade them.

A woman kisses another woman on the cheek, but we don't actually see it (28).

A woman impulsively kisses an older man on the forehead (41).

A woman and a man are about to kiss, but are interrupted (42).

A woman and a man indulge in a long kiss, but it is obscured by the man's back (46).

A woman and a man kiss on a few different occasions, seen once from the side (lips actually meet, for once), other times from the back only (50).

Restaurants and bars

There are eating and drinking establishments in almost every Ozu film (in fact, it's hard to think of an exception; one might be 39, the first post-war film, in which a little feast is held at home), and some of them are frequented in more than one film. Obviously, it all takes place in the studio, not in actual bars or restaurants. Here are a few examples.

The same eel restaurant is seen twice (47, 51), first the sign outside then the identical interior, also with the same waitress in both films.

Luna Bar is visited in two films (48, 51), with the same sign outside, same interior and the same barman. The Luna sign is also seen—implausibly—through the window of a second-floor restaurant during a class reunion (53).

Wakamatsu Restaurant, with the same proprietress, slightly ridiculed by the male customers, is visited in three films (48, 51, 53).

Girls at work

Young women in their early or late twenties are seen in many films working as house maids (mainly in pre-war films), hotel maids, restaurant waitresses, and bar hostesses, but there is also a considerable repetition of the roll of a young woman working in an office of a large company. These can be divided into two types:

Surprisingly often, she works as an English typist (20, 27, 28, 43, 46), or stenographer (41), or studying stenography (47).

In other cases, she does some more routine desk work, or shows visitors into offices (45, 47, 51, 52, 53).

In a few cases we know that a girl works in a company, but we don't get to see her at work (37, 48, 49, 53).

Fun and games

Baseball—played by children or adults (36, 41, 43, 52), and at the ballpark (44, 53).

Bicycle races (44, 52).

Billiards (27, 28).

Boxing (27, 28).

Fishing (31, 38, 50).

Go (38, 43, 53).

Golf (14, 36, 48, 51, 53).

Mahjong (40, 45, 46, 47, 51).

Pachinko (44, 47)—in the former Ryū Chishū owns a parlor, in the later he plays in one.

Shōgi (25, 31, 50).

Names

Following are some of the names repeated across the films (*=characters played by Ryū Chishū).

Family names:

> Hirayama (*44, *45, 46, 48, 51, *53).
>
> Sugiyama (36, 46, *47, 50, 51).

Men's names:

> Kihachi (29, 31, 32, 33, 39)—all played by Sakamoto Takeshi.
>
> Kōichi (*43, 45, 46, 51, 52, 53).
>
> Shūkichi (*41, *45, *47, 48, 43, *51, 51—also a second character).

Women's names

> Names with O are pre-war, names with -ko are mostly post-war):
>
> Akiko (40, 41, 47, 48, 51, 52).

Aya—The modern girlfriend of the heroin (41, 43, 44); Ayako (37, 40, 51).

Noriko—Three times it is Hara Setsuko's character (41, 43, 45), once her sister-in-law (52).

Setsuko—Usually the young daughter or a niece (36, 37, 42, 44, 48, 49).

Shige (alternatively Oshige, Shigeko)—usually maids, older sisters, and wives (25, 37, 39, 41, 43, 44, 46, 47, 49, 50, 51, 52).

Tsune or Otsune (29, 31, 35, 40, 47, 52)—the first three roles are played by Iida Chōko.

Names of children after the war:

Isamu (43, 45, 49), the younger son.

Minoru (43, 45, 49, 52), the older or only son.

The old teacher

Former classmates, even middle-aged men, often get together with one or two of their teachers for a nostalgic class reunion around tables laid out with food and drinks. However, in three films the once respected and even feared teacher now makes a living running a modest restaurant (22, 35, 53). In another case, he works as a supervisor in a factory (38).

Commemorative photographs

Formally facing the camera for a photograph commemorating an important life event or a visit to some famous site is a long-established Japanese tradition. Ozu used it several times, often with some particular significance in the story (37, 38, 39, 43, 51, 53).

Children studying English

Doing their homework or being tutored, children struggle with the foreign language in at least four films (37, 38, 45, 49). Further, in two of these films, which have a time gap of eighteen years (37 & 49), the almost exact same sentence is being translated ("my [younger] sister is three years younger than me"). Indeed, English language education in Japan has not made much progress over the decades.

Books

Apart from children doing their homework, there are a few scenes in which someone is seen reading a book (or trying to read, but being interrupted in 38, 51). However, in many films, bookcases are seen in the background. There are often large, distinguish-looking books (probably at least partially foreign), seen in apartments where they might not necessarily be expected, or not looking like they are actually being read (35, 45 and several others).

Sewing

Women, and at least in one case a man (38), are seen sewing, usually mending clothes, in many films. There is one common denominator: whenever people are seen sewing, at one point they would scratch their head with the top of the needle.

Select Actors' Profiles

The following short profiles include many of Ozu's regular actors, as well as some who had a particularly memorable appearance in one, two or three of his films, arranged alphabetically. To save space, in some cases films are indicated by their numbers on the attached list rather than by their full title. As was once common in Hollywood, Japanese studios also gave their potential stars a catchy name; the original names are indicated.

Aoki Hōhi (born c. 1924)

A child actor who appeared in Ozu's first three post-war films (39, 40, 41). He was a half-brother of Aoki Tomio, better remembered as Tokkan Kozō (see below), but unlike him, his own career in film was short.

Aratama Michiyo (1930–2001)

Real name Toda Kyōko. Starting her career in the Takarazuka Review before turning to film, she became a leading star in the Japanese cinema of the 1950's and 60's. Later she gave up films in favor of the stage and television dramas. Like several other female stars of her time, as well as some older ones (such as Awashima Chikage, Hara Setsuko, and Tanaka Kinuyo), she never married and had no children. In her only appearance in an Ozu film, she made a memorable impression as the strong-willed elder daughter of the family in *The End of Summer* (1961).

Arima Ineko (1932–)

Real name Nakanishi Mitsuko. As a child, she was taken from her biological parents and adopted by an aunt who lived in Korea, reuniting unhappily with her parents after the war. She joined the Takarazuka Review School in 1949 and had her film debut in 1951. She had a long career in film and on stage, and was last seen on both the large and small screens in 2019. She married and divorced twice and had no children. For Ozu, she twice played the "difficult" daughter in *Tokyo Twilight* (1957) and *Equinox Flower* (1958).

Awashima Chikage (1924–2012)

Real name Nakagawa Keiko. Like Aratama and Arima (above), Awashima also started in the Takarazuka Review before turning to film in 1950. A leading star of her time, she had a long career in film and television almost until the end of her life. She had three memorable roles in Ozu's films, twice as the protagonist's friend Aya, in *Early Summer* (1951) and *The Flavor of Green Tea over Rice* (1952), and then in a leading role as the betrayed wife who is willing to give her marriage another chance in *Early Spring* (1956).

Date Satoko (1910–1972)

Real name Ishikawa Mie. Trying in various ways to fulfil her dream of becoming a film actress, she was eventually recruited in 1929 by Shōchiku on the recommendation of script writer and Ozu's collaborator Noda Kōgo, who was her relative. She soon became the very model of the contemporary *moga* (modern girl) in a long list of films. In 1931, she participated in Japan's first feature-length talking film, *The Neighbor's Wife and Mine* alongside Tanaka

Kinuyo. She later became a free agent, appeared on the stage, and her film career lasted until the early 1950's. In 1951, she married Tasaki Hanama, and American-born Japanese who was in Japan during the war and later published two bestseller novels. After their divorce, she was baptized Catholic. She played the assertive *moga* in five Ozu films, two of which are lost (17, 26), and three where her performance can be enjoyed (14, 20, 25).

Egawa Ureo (1902–1970)

He was born in Japan to a Japanese mother and a German father, "Ureo" being a Japanese pronunciation of his German name, Willy. For a while he was a member of a gang of delinquents before finding work in films. He had outstanding leading roles in *Where Now Are the Dreams of Youth?* (1932) and *Woman of Tokyo* (1933) and reappeared as a distinguished white-haired man in a class reunion in *Equinox Flower* (1958).

Hara Setsuko (1920–2015)

Ozu's best-known actress was also one of Japan's most loved screen actresses ever. With a face full of character and an accepting smile, she had an unmistakable style uniquely her own. In spite of a relatively short career of 27 years, she left a lasting impact on the history of Japanese cinema.

Her real name was Aida Masae, and she was given her screen name by the studio, at her debut, aged 15. Between 1935 and 1962 she appeared in 101 films. She was probably the most popular actress in Japan for many years, nicknamed *eien no madonna*, "the eternal virgin," because she never married or had children in real life, although on the screen she often portrayed wives or mothers. Hara appeared in the films of several famous Japanese directors, and also in one film directed by a foreigner, the German director of "mountain films" Arnold Fanck, who included her in his German-Japanese production, known in English as *The New Earth* (1937).

During the Second World War she appeared in many nationalistic and militaristic films, but that did not stop her from portraying soon after the war the wife of a dissident in *No Regrets For Our Youth* by Kurosawa Akira (who himself directed two or three propaganda-filled films during the war). She also appeared in Kurosawa's *Idiot*, a failed attempt at adopting Dostoyevsky's novel, perhaps due to cuts imposed by the studio.

Hara appeared in sixty-one films before participating for the first time in an Ozu film, and later had parts in thirty-four other films apart from the six under his direction, but she is best remembered—at least outside Japan—for the figure created during this famous collaboration between director and actress. A short while after Ozu's death, although not openly connecting between the two events, she announced her retirement from the screen at age forty-three, to the shock and dismay of the Japanese public. To add insult to injury, she even said that she did not really like acting in films, and that she did it mostly in order to support her family, and now that they were taken care of, there was no reason for her to go on working. She went into secluded life in a small house in Kamakura, resolutely avoiding the public and the media. She even refused to participate in a documentary dedicated to Ozu's work, in which many of his collaborators appeared.

In spite of her long retirement, in a list of "Film Stars of the Twentieth Century" published by the leading Japanese film magazine *Kinema Junpo* in 2000, Hara was elected first place among Japanese film actresses.

Hara's six portrayals of women in Ozu's film are neatly divided down the middle: in the first three, termed "the Noriko trilogy" by later critics, she played a daughter who must get married (twice) or a widowed daughter-in-law. After a hiatus of four years she reappeared and played the role of a mother (widowed or separated from her husband) in three other films. These films are as follows (the age of the characters is according to the scripts):

Late Spring (1949)

Somiya Noriko (27), the only daughter of a widowed professor, who wishes to go on living with her father, but eventually agrees to an arranged marriage.

Early Summer (1951)

Mamiya Noriko (28), the youngest daughter in the family, who, under pressure to agree to an arranged marriage, chooses her spouse without the family's consent. Works as a typist in a Tokyo company.

Tokyo Story (1953)

Hirayama Noriko (28), widow of the second son of the family, who died in the war. Supports herself as an office worker in Tokyo, and treats her elderly in-laws with kindness.

Tokyo Twilight (1957)

Numata Takako (32), the elder of two sisters, who leaves her drunken husband and goes with her baby daughter to stay with her father. Eventually she decides to attempt a reconciliation.

Late Autumn (1960)

Miwa Akiko (45), a widowed mother who wishes to see her 24 years old daughter married. Works as a sewing teacher.

The End Of Summer (1961)

Kohayakawa Akiko (37), the widow of the family's elder son, mother to a young boy, who prefers not to remarry. Works in an art gallery.

Higashiyama Chieko (1890–1980)

Real name Kōno Sen. Starting her distinguished stage career (especially in Chekhov plays) as late as when she was thirty-five and long married to a businessman with whom she lived in Moscow before the October Revolution, she had many roles in films and television, including two memorable parts in Ozu's films: Ryū Chishū's mother in *Early Summer* (1951), and his wife in *Tokyo Story* (1953).

Iida Chōko (1897–1972)

Iida was Ozu's most constant actress during the silent era, and up to his first post-war film. She came from a poor background, joined Shōchiku in 1923, and went on to act until the last year of her life, appearing in some 300 films and television dramas. In Ozu's films she often played characters who displayed a combination of softness and toughness, caring but standing her ground.

She married Shigehara Hideo, known usually as Mohara Hideo, who was Ozu's main cinematographer in the 1920's and 30's, and who also developed a sound system which Ozu used when he started making talkies.

Several of Iida's Ozu films are fully or partially lost (6, 7, 10, 26, 29, 32, 34), and in some of the surviving ones she had small, although often memorable roles (8, 20, 22, 25, 37). Among her outstanding roles are:

Story of Floating Weeds (1934)

Otsune, a restaurant owner who was the long-ago lover of the actor Kihachi and is the mother of his son.

An Inn in Tokyo (1935)

Otsune, a restaurant owner who helps Kihachi and his children.

The Only Son (1936)

Finally in a leading role as Nonomiya Tsune (Otsune), the mother who sacrificed so much for her son's education but is disappointed at what has become of him.

What Did the Lady Forget? (1937)

Here she is in the atypical role of a high society lady, Ushigume Chiyoko, who often enjoys the hospitality of her friend, the doctor's wife. For once she is out of the traditional kimono and the humble environment and into fashionable dresses and luxurious cars.

Record of a Tenement Gentleman (1947)

Otane, a widowed shopkeeper who takes care of a lost boy against her wishes, but develops feelings for him and is sorry to let him go.

Ikebe Ryō (1918–2010)

He joined Tōhō in 1941, and after serving in the Pacific War, gained popularity in the late 1940's as a youth idol. He often appeared in *yakuza* and other genre films, but his range was wide and his list of movie and television drama roles is extremely long. In his later years he was also a reputed writer. Shōchiku rarely allowed Ozu to hire from outside the studio, so Ikebe appeared only in *Early Spring* (1956) in a very memorable leading role.

Iwashita Shima (1941–)

Had her film debut in 1960 while still a student, and the same year had a small part as an office worker in *Late Autumn*. She went on to have a long career on stage and television as well as in films, and was outstanding in the role of Ryū's daughter Michiko in *An Autumn Afternoon* (1962). In 1967 she married film director Shinoda Masahiro (his second marriage), and appeared in many of his films.

Kagawa Kyōko (1931–)

In 1949 she was discovered in a "New Face Nomination" contest and had her debut the following year. She went on to have an extremely long and distinguished career in film and television, appearing in some of the classic films of Mizoguchi, Kurosawa and others. She won many prizes and distinctions in Japan, and was still acting in her eighties. She was in only one Ozu film, playing the young daughter in *Tokyo Story* (1953). At the time she expressed her happiness of playing opposite Hara Setsuko, whom she greatly admired.

Katō Daisuke (1911–1975)

Born to the Sawamura theatrical family, he acted in films from 1936, but changed his screen name after serving in the Pacific War and signing with Daiei Film, later moving to Tōhō. He appeared in over 200 films, many by the most distinguished Japanese directors, including four of Kurosawa Akira's films (*Rashomon, Seven Samurai*, *Ikiru* and *Yojimbo*). His son Haruyuki married Kurosawa's daughter Kazuko. His sister Sawamura Sadako also appeared in two of Ozu's films, while he appeared in three: twice as a war veteran who gets drunk on saké and memories, in *Early Spring* (1956) and *An Autumn Afternoon* (1962), and once as a family member in *The End of Summer* (1961).

Kishi Keiko (1932–)

She had her debut in 1951, and stared in many Japanese and a few foreign films (such as Sydney Pollack's *The Yakuza*). In 1957 she married French director Yves Ciampi and commuted for a while between Paris and Japan. They had one daughter and divorced in 1975. Her latest role was in a 2019 television drama. She was outstanding in the role of the protagonist's spurned lover in *Early Spring* (1956), although years later she said that when asking the director why she had to repeat her scenes so many times, Ozu's answer was: "because you are such an incompetent actress." In fact, Ozu required all his actors to repeat their scenes again and again until he was satisfied.

Kishida Kyōko (1930–2006)

The daughter of the distinguished playwright and director Kishida Kunio, she started her career on stage and later moved on to film and television, gaining great respect in all media. She expressed her regret for appearing in only one of Ozu's films, as the "Madam" of a bar in *An Autumn Afternoon* (1962) (see more above under that film).

Kita Ryūji (1905–1972)

Real name Yamada Tōgo. Hired by Shōchiku as a script writer, he started acting in 1937, appearing in hundreds of films and television dramas up to his final year. He had three quite similar parts in the same number of Ozu's films. In *Equinox Flower* (1958) his character was called *Horie*, one of the friends of the protagonist (called *Hirayama* and played by Saburi Shin; other friends are played by Nakamura Nobuo, called *Kawai*, and Ryū Chishū). In *Late Autumn* he was Professor *Hirayama*, one of the three friends of the family (together with Saburi Shin and Nakamura Nobuo), a widower who wishes to marry the character played by Hara Setsuko. In *An Autumn Afternoon* he was again called *Horie*, one of three friends (together with Nakamura Nobuo called *Kawai* again, and Ryū Chishū, who once again assumed the name of *Hirayama*), a widowed professor who has recently acquired a young wife. In both latter films he is being ridiculed by his friends.

Kogure Michiyo (1918–1990)

Real name Wada Tsuma. She joined Shōchiku in 1938 while still a university student and had a long and distinguished career as a particularly versatile actress. In 1944 she married a cousin 20 years her senior and went with him to Manchuria, repatriating two years later. She resumed her film career in 1947, and worked for other studios besides Shōchiku, appearing in the films of Kurosawa, Mizoguchi, Naruse and many other directors. For Ozu she acted in only one film, as the wife who reconciles with her husband in *The Flavor of Green Tea over Rice* (1952).

Kurishima Sumiko (1902-1987)

She was trained as a traditional dancer from a young age, but in 1921 joined Shōchiku and was considered Japan's first female movie star. She retired from the screen in 1938 to focus on her dancing, returning only once, to appear in Naruse's film *Flowing* (1956), in which several other actresses and some actors familiar from Ozu's films participated. Kurishima was married to film director and executive Ikeda Yoshinobu. For Ozu she acted in two lost films (13, 19), and received top billing in *What did the Lady Forget?* (1937).

Kuwano Michiko (1915–1946) and Kuwano Miyuki (1942–)

Kuwano Michiko's promising career was cut short at the age of thirty-one when she collapsed on a film set. She had a very memorable part in *What did the Lady Forget?* (1937) as Setsuko, the modern and unruly niece from Osaka. She also had a smaller part in *The Brothers and Sisters of the Toda Family* (1941) as Tokiko, the working-class friend of the youngest Toda sister. She left behind her daughter Miyuki, who appeared in many films from 1954 until her marriage and retirement in 1967. In Ozu's films she had two small parts as a sassy teenaged daughter in *Equinox Flower* (1958) and *An Autumn Afternoon* (1962). In between she gained notoriety for her role in Ōshima Nagisa's *Cruel Story of Youth* (1960), which was a harbinger of the so-called Japanese New Wave, representing the exact opposite of Ozu's cinema in every aspect.

Kyō Machiko (1924–2019)

Real name Yano Motoko. Entering the stage as a revue dancer aged twelve, she gained certain international fame for her role as the samurai's wife in Kurosawa Akira's *Rashomon* (1950), and then in the Hollywood film *The Teahouse of the August Moon* (1956). She appeared in several other classic films by leading Japanese directors, was considered one of Japan's biggest stars of the 1950's and 60's, and was active through to her 80's. She never married, but was known to have had a long romantic relationship with the president of Daiei Film, Nagata Masaichi, the same man who cut short the film career of Yamamoto Fujiko (see below), and may have been responsible for the suicide of Marui Tarō, who had a small part in *Floating Weeds* (1959), the same film in which Kyō Machiko exceled herself in the role of Sumiko, the leading actress of the traveling troop and the mistress of its leader.

Mitsui Kōji (Hideo) (1910–1979)

He joined Shōchiku at 14 and had parts in many silent films. He changed studios a few times, appeared on the stage, and was considered a valuable character actor, appearing also in several of Kurosawa Akira's films. Due to his drinking and health problems, in later life he appeared mostly on television. He was in seven Ozu films over a period of twenty-six years, among them one partially lost (30), and two in which he had but small parts (38, 40). His memorable roles are:

Dragnet Girl (1933)

Hiroshi, a student and a fledgling boxer who joins the criminal gang, but later wishes to reform.

Story of Floating Weeds (1934)

Shinkichi, the young man who finds out that he is the son of the head of the actors' troop.

Early Spring (1956)

Hirayama, a war time friend of the protagonist.

Floating Weeds (1959)

Kichinosuke, an actor in the visiting troop. He is the only actor who appeared in both versions of the film.

Miyake Kuniko (1916–1992)

Real name Miura Yasu. She had her screen debut in 1934 and appeared in hundreds of films and television dramas until late in her life. One of the most familiar faces in Ozu's films, she had small or supporting roles in nine of them.

The Brothers and Sisters of the Toda Family (1941)

Kazuko, the wife of the eldest son of the Toda family, a mother of one.

Late Spring (1949)

Miwa Akiko (38), a widow and the father's prospective bride.

Early Summer (1951)

Mamiya Fumiko (35), the wife of the eldest son (Ryū Chishū), a mother of two.

The Flavor of Green Tea over Rice (1952)

Yamauchi Chizu (42), Taeko's sister in law, a mother of two.

Tokyo Story (1953)

Hirayama Fumiko (39), the wife of the eldest son, a mother of two.

Early Spring (1956)

Yukiko, the wife of Kawai Yutaka, "Blue Mountain" café/bar owner.

Good Morning (1959)

Hayashi Tamiko (37), wife of Keitarō (Ryū Chishū), a mother of two.

Late Autumn (1960)

Taguchi Nobuko (46), wife of Shūzō (Nakamura Nobuo), a mother of two.

An Autumn Afternoon (1962)

Kawai Nobuko (46), wife of Shūzō (Nakamura Nobuo).

Nakamura Ganjirō (1902–1983)

In fact, he was Nakamura Ganjirō II, taking the name of his father as is the tradition in the kabuki theater, and followed by his son, Ganjirō III, and grandson, Ganjirō IV. After long years as a distinguished actor in the kabuki theater, in an uncommon move he turned to the cinema from 1957, appearing in many films throughout the following decade, and occasionaly later too. In Ozu's films he had two memorable parts: as Arashi Komajurō, the head of the actors' troop in *Floating Weeds* (1959), and as Kohayakawa Manbei, the head of the family in *The End of Summer* (1961).

Nakamura Nobuo (1908–1991)

A distinguished stage actor, he started appearing in films in the 1950's and was still seen on the screen in the late 1980's. Apart from Ozu's he was in other important directors' films, including Kurosawa Akira and Naruse Mikio. A familiar face in Ozu's late films, he appeared in six of them:

Tokyo Story (1953)

Kaneko Kurazō (49), the husband of the eldest daughter Shige.

Early Spring (1956)

Arakawa (52), company department head, Shōji's boss.

Tokyo Twilight (1957)

Aijima Sakae (54), the husband of the estranged mother.

Equinox Flower (1958)

Kawai Toshihiko (55), whose daughter's wedding reception the Hirayamas attend.

Late Autumn (1960)

Taguchi Shūzō (54), family friend.

An Autumn Afternoon (1961)

Kawai Shūzō (57), Hirayama's old friend and Michiko's boss.

Okada Tokihiko (1903–1934) and Okada Mariko (1933–)

Okada Tokihiko's real name was Takahashi Eiichi. Having had his debut in 1920, Okada's brilliant career as a leading star of the silent era was cut short by his death due to tuberculosis at the age of thirty. Not only good looking, he was also a very accomplished actor. He was a friend of Ozu and appeared in five of his films, two of which are lost (19, 21). However, it is a real pleasure watching him in the leading roles in the other three films: *That Night's Wife* (1930), *The Lady and the Beard*, and especially *Tokyo Chorus* (both 1931). He married Tazuru Sonoko, a star of the Takarazuka Review, and their only daughter Mariko was one year old when he died.

Mariko, who was raised by her mother's sister while the mother was working as a dance teacher in China, had her film debut aged seventeen at Tōhō, where she appeared in several films by Naruse Mikio, before moving to Shōchiku. She later married film director Yoshida Yoshishige and appeared in many of his films. She also appeared on the stage and in television dramas. For Ozu, from whom she learned about her father, she acted in two memorable roles: as Yuriko in *Late Autumn* (1960), and as Akiko in *An Autumn Afternoon* (1962).

Okada Yoshiko (1902–1992)

She was a stage actress from 1919, and had her film debut in 1923, in both cases helping to break the taboo of allowing women to appear before the public. She became a film star, but her career was derailed for a while due to a romantic scandal. In 1932 she joined Shōchiku and appeared, among others, in three Ozu films. However, in early 1938 she defected to the Soviet Union with her lover. During the 1939 purges, he was executed and she was imprisoned until 1947. She returned to Japan in 1972 and resumed her stage and film careers, but returned to Moscow in 1986, where she died. Among her Ozu films, one is lost (26) but she can be seen in *Woman of Tokyo* (1933) and *An Inn in Tokyo* (1935).

Ryū Chishū (1904–1993)

The actor most identified as the Ozu persona was the son of a Buddhist priest from Kyushu. He was expected to take his father's place, but opted for acting, in which he had an extremely long career, spanning sixty-five years and several hundred films. Although he worked with many other directors, Ryū himself recognized that it was Ozu who formed him and made him the skillful actor that he was. (See more under *An Autumn Afternoon* above).

Ryū was also an accomplished reciter and singer in some traditional Japanese genres. His first recorded singing must have been in *There was a Father*, but that part of the film no longer exists. He can be heard performing in *Record of a Tenement Gentleman*, *The Flavor of Green Tea over Rice*, and *Equinox Flower*.

According to Ryū, he was in all of Ozu films but two (21 and 36). This cannot be verified because so many early films are lost, and in many cases he only had walk-on parts or very small roles, such as—in the surviving films—one of the students (8, 22), a policeman (16, 28, 33), an employee handling the projector (24), a reporter (27), a man on boat (29), and a man shouting in the theater (31). He gradually received more substantial parts, including in one of the lost films (34). Following is a list of all his other roles (the age of the characters is according to the scripts):

I Flunked, But . . . (1930)

Hattori, one of the students who graduated, probably his first credited role in an Ozu film.

Where Now Are the Dreams of Youth? (1932)

Shimazaki Shōgo, a student, later company employee, one of the four friends.

The Only Son (1936)

Ōkubo, the rural teacher who ends up running a restaurant in suburban Tokyo.

The Brothers and Sisters of the Toda Family (1941)

Inoue, one of two friends of the younger son, seen in one scene only.

There was a Father (1942)

The father, Horikawa Shūhei, his first leading role.

Record of a Tenement Gentleman (1947)

Tashiro, a fortune teller who brings the lost boy to the tenement.

A Hen in the Wind (1948)

Satake Waichirō, Shūichi's employer.

Late Spring (1949)

Somiya Shūkichi (56), the father, professor at Tokyo University.

The Munakata Sisters (1950)

Munakata Tadachika (60), the father of the two sisters, retired in Kyoto.

Early Summer (1951)

Mamiya Kōichi (38), the elder son, a medical doctor.

The Flavor of Green Tea over Rice (1952)

Hirayama Sadao (42), pachinko parlor owner, served under Mokichi in the war.

Tokyo Story (1953)

Hirayama Shūkichi (70), the old father.

Early Spring (1956)

Onodera Kiichi (45), Sugiyama's friend, widower, employed by the same company in Ōtsu.

Tokyo Twilight (1957)

Sugiyama Shūkichi (57), a bank auditor, the father of the two sisters.

Equinox Flower (1958)

Mikami Shūkichi (56), Hirayama's old friend whose daughter left home.

Good Morning (1959)

Hayashi Keitarō (46), company employee, father of two boys.

Floating Weeds (1959)

Aioi Theater owner (57), has one scene.

Late Autumn (1960)

Miwa Shūkichi (59), Akiko's brother-in-law, an inn keeper, seen in two scenes.

The End of Summer (1961)

A farmer (57), has one scene.

An Autumn Afternoon (1962)

Hirayama Shūhei (57), company executive, the father.

Saburi Shin (1909–1982)

Real name Yoshizaki Yoshio. His debut was in 1931, and from the mid-1930's he became one of Shōchiku's biggest male stars, appearing in the films of many leading directors. In 1950 he also started to direct, first films and later television dramas. In Ozu's films we can see him advance from the young and reckless son to the mature company executive, always mixing the serious with the slightly comical. His five roles were as follows:

The Brothers and Sisters of the Toda Family (1941)

Shōjirō, the son who reprimands his elder siblings for the way they treated their mother.

There was a Father (1942)

Kurokawa Yasutarō, one of the graduates who arrange a party for their teachers.

The Flavor of Green Tea over Rice

Satake Mokichi (42), the husband with simple tastes.

Equinox Flower (1958)

Hirayama Wataru (55), company executive, the father who opposes his daughter's choice.

Late Autumn (1960)

Mamiya Sōichi (54), company executive and family friend.

Sada Keiji (1926–1964)

Real name Nakai Kan'ichi. His film debut was in 1947, and he soon turned into one of Japan's biggest male stars of the 1950's and early 1960's. He had a particularly close relationship with Ozu, whom he regarded as a father figure. He took care of him during his illness and broke down when he died. His wife Mashiko was formerly Ozu's secretary. He was also close to director Kinoshita Keisuke. Tragically, he was killed in a car accident when his driver collided with another car. His wife and two children who were also in the car were unharmed. Both children, a boy and girl, later became film actors. He had parts in four Ozu films:

Equinox Flower (1958)

Taniguchi Masahiko (32), a company employee who becomes Setsuko's fiancé against her father's wish.

Good Morning (1959)

Fukui Heiichirō (29), unemployed, translates and teaches English at home, love interest of Setsuko.

Late Autumn (1960)

Gotō Shōtarō (31), a company employee, Ayako's marriage prospect.

An Autumn Afternoon (1962)

Hirayama Kōichi (32), the eldest son, a company employee, Akiko's husband.

Saitō Tatsuo (1902–1968)

He made his film debut in 1925 and had a long and distinguished career up to the last year of his life. With Sakamoto Takeshi, Saitō was one of the two most frequently appearing actors in Ozu's films in the pre-war era, appearing in some of the most memorable leading roles in Ozu's silent films. As he would later do with Ryū Chishū, when not cast in a leading role Ozu would include him in some minor role or in a short cameo. However, like Sakamoto, after appearing in one post-war film (Sakamoto was in two), Ozu did not cast him again. He appeared in twenty-four of the director's films, of which thirteen are lost or mostly lost (2, 3, 4, 6, 11, 12, 13, 17, 18, 19, 21, 23, 34). His surviving roles are as follows:

Days of Youth (1929)

Yamamoto Shuichi, one of the two students in the leading roles.

Walk Cheerfully (1930)

Man in the billiard parlor.

I Flunked, But . . . (1930)

Takahashi, the student who leads the flunkies.

That Night's Wife (1930)

Doctor Sugita.

The Lady and the Beard (1931)

Head of the opponent kendo team.

Tokyo Chorus (1931)

Ōmura, the teacher who helps his former student to find a job.

I Was Born, But . . . (1932)

Yoshii Kennosuke, an office worker, the father who loses his sons' respect.

Where Now Are the Dreams of Youth? (1932)

Saiki Taichiō, student, later company employee who angers his boss and former friend.

What Did the Lady Forget? (1937)

Doctor Komiya, a professor of medicine, the intimidated husband.

The Brothers and Sisters of the Toda Family (1941)

Shinichirō, the elder son.

The Munakata Sisters (1950)

Uchida Yuzuru (59), professor of medicine in Kyoto.

Sakamoto Takeshi (1899–1974)

Real name Nagaishi Buhei. With the exception of Ryū Chishū, Sakamoto was Ozu's most frequent actor, appearing in twent-five films, mostly of the pre-war era. A prolific comic actor, he is reputed to have acted in some 300 films and television dramas from his 1923 debut until the mid-1960's. For Ozu he played many minor or supporting roles before advancing to the main role as Kihachi in four films (one of them is lost). In these major roles, as in many minor ones, he gave unforgettable comic and sometimes very touching performances. He also had minor roles in Ozu's first two post-war films.

He had parts in eleven lost or mostly lost films (2, 3, 4, 6, 10, 11, 12, 18, 23, 32, 34). His roles in the surviving films are as follows:

Days of Youth (1929)

Professor.

Walk Cheerfully (1930)

Ono, the lascivious company manager.

The Lady and the Beard (1931)

The rich family's butler.

Tokyo Chorus (1931)

The elderly company employee, Yamada, who is being fired.

I Was Born, But . . . (1932)

The father's boss, Iwasaki Sōhei.

Where Now Are the Dreams of Youth? (1932)

The Horino family's butler.

Passing Fancy (1933)

Kihachi, a day laborer.

Story of Floating Weeds (1934)

Kihachi (Ichikawa Sahanji), the head of a troop of actors.

An Inn in Tokyo (1935)

Kihachi, a day laborer.

What Did the Lady Forget? (1937)

Ushigume executive, Sugiyama, a golfing friend of the doctor.

The Brothers and Sisters of the Toda Family (1941)

Antique dealer, one scene.

There was a Father (1942)

Hirata Makoto, a teacher in Kanazawa, later met in Tokyo, the father's friend.

Record of a Tenement Gentleman (1947)

Kawayoshi Kihachi, head of the neighborhood group, a dyer.

A Hen in the Wind (1948)

Sakai Hikozō, Tokiko's landlord.

Sugawara Tsūsai (1894–1981)

Viewers of Ozu's later films would have noticed an elderly, burly gentleman, with a somewhat rectangular head, sipping saké in a bar while making some terse comments, or otherwise appearing for just a moment or two, only to reappear in the following film. This man was not an actor, but a prominent industrialist and real estate developer, known also as "the fixer," for his involvement in public policy and his backing of politicians of various parties. He was also known as a social reformer and a patron of the arts. A friend of Ozu's, the director arranged for him to play cameo roles in six of his final seven films. He appears as a bar or a restaurant customer (46, 49, 51), a mahjong player neglecting his work (47), a man in a class reunion (48, 53), and an antique dealer (50). In the scripts he is usually named "Sugai," which is a shortened version of his full name.

Sugimura Haruko (1909–1997)

Real name Ishiyama Haruko. She was one of Japan's greatly admired actresses and was considered by Ozu as a particularly important collaborator. Starting as a stage actress in 1927, she continued to appear on the stage until her retirement in 1996. Her film debut was in 1932, and she had parts in many films, later also in television dramas. Apart from Ozu, she was a favorite actress of Naruse Mikio. She received numerous awards in Japan, for both her stage and screen work.

In Ozu's films she usually played the energetic, fast-talking, sometimes interfering—or even insensitive—daughter, neighbor or aunt, although in a few cases she had more subdued parts. She had memorable roles in nine post-war films:

Late Spring (1949)

Taguchi Masa (49), the father's sister, who arranges Noriko's wedding.

Early Summer (1951)

Yabe Tami (54), the mother of the doctor, who asks Noriko to marry her son.

Tokyo Story (1953)

Kaneko Shige (44), the Hirayamas' elder daughter, a beautician.

Early Spring (1956)

Tamura Tamako (45), the Sugiyamas' neighbor across the alley.

Tokyo Twilight (1957)

Takeuchi Shigeko (46), the father's sister, owns a cosmetic products company, trying to arrange a marriage for her niece.

Good Morning (1959)

Haraguchi Kikue (38), neighborhood wife.

Floating Weeds (1959)

Honma Oyoshi (45), Tsuruya restaurant proprietress and former lover of the lead actor.

The End of Summer (1961)

Kato Shige (48), Manbei sister from Nagoya.

An Autumn Afternoon (1963)

Sakuma Tomoko (48), the unmarried daughter of the old teacher.

Takahashi Toyo (1903–1981)

She started her career as a stage actress, joined Shōchiku in 1946, and was active in film and television dramas until the late 1970's. Hers was a familiar face in Ozu's post-war films, albeit in small roles and often ridiculed.

Late Spring (1949)

Hayashi Shige (44), the help at Somiya's house.

Early Summer (1951)

Aya's mother Nobu (52), Tamura Restaurant proprietress.

Tokyo Story (1953)

Hirayama's neighbor, passing by the house at the beginning and the end of the film.

Equinox Flower (1958)

Wakamatsu Restaurant proprietress.

Good Morning (1959)

Ōkubo Shige (40), neighborhood housewife

Floating Weeds (1959)

Barber's intimidating wife

Late Autumn (1960)

Wakamatsu Restaurant proprietress (50).

An Autumn Afternoon (1962)

Wakamatsu Restaurant proprietress.

Takamine Hideko (1924–2010)

She became a popular child actress from the age of five, and her career spanned some fifty years. In the 1950's she was considered Japan's top star, due to her roles in immensely popular films by Kinoshita Keisuke and Naruse Mikio. In 1955 she married screenwriter and director Matsuyama Zensō, but continued working. She was active on the screen until 1979, and later published several books, having started publishing essays in the 1950's. In Ozu's films she first appeared as the young daughter in *Tokyo Chorus* (1931), and years later as the younger sibling in *The Munakata Sisters* (1950).

Takamine Mieko (1918–1990)

She came from a musical family, and had her film debut in 1936, soon becoming famous as both an actress and a singer. A major star of the 1940's and 1950's, her career lasted until the last year of her life. She appeared in only one Ozu films, as the young sister in *The Brothers and Sisters of the Toda Family* (1941).

Tanaka Kinuyo (1910–1977)

Regarded as one of the greatest actresses in the history of Japanese cinema, her first appearance was in 1924, during the silent film era, and her last in 1976, and throughout these more than fifty years on the screen she appeared in some 250 films. She is best known as the favorite actress of director Mizoguchi Kenji, appearing in fifteen of his films including the leading roles in great classics such as *The Life of Oharu* (1952) and *Ugetsu* (1953). She also appeared in the films of many other directors, including Kurosawa Akira, for whom she acted in *Red Beard* (1965).

Tanaka was also the second woman director in Japanese film history. She directed six feature films between 1953 and 1961, including *The Moon Has Risen* (1955), based on a script given to her by Ozu, and with the participation of Ryū Chishū, Ozu's favorite actor. A dramatization of her life, *Actress* (1987), was directed by the famous Ichikawa Kon, staring Yoshinaga Sayuri.

Tanaka was one of the few actors or actresses who appeared in both Ozu's early silent films as well as his late post-war classics. Ozu tended to cast her in submissive roles, but her inner fire could always be felt behind the submissiveness (physical violence is rare in Ozu's post-war films, but Tanaka got beaten or slapped by her husbands in two of them). She appeared in nine of Ozu's films:

I Graduated, But . . . (1929, mostly lost)

Machiko, the wife of the unemployed protagonist, starts working in a bar.

I Flunked, But . . . (1930)

Café girl with whom the students flirt.

Young Miss (1930, lost)

Kinuko, the girlfriend of one of the protagonists.

Where Now Are the Dreams of Youth? (1932)

Oshige, bakery girl near the university, later marries one of the former students.

Woman of Tokyo (1933)

Harue, girlfriend of the protagonist.

Dragnet Girl (1933)

Tokiko, girlfriend of the gang boss, who also works as a typist.

A Hen In The Wind (1948)

Amamiya Tokiko, the wife who prostitutes herself to pay for her son's hospital bills while her husband is conscripted.

The Munakata Sisters (1950)

Setsuko, the elder of the two sisters, whose husband drinks and is violent.

Equinox Flower (1958)

Hirayama Kiyoko, the wife who is trying to help her daughter marry the man she loves in spite of her husband's objections.

Tokkan Kozō (1923–2004)

Real name Aoki Tomio. Ozu started using him when he was six, and was so impressed by his abilities, that he made a short film as a vehicle specifically for him, and the boy was so much identified with the role that he adopted it as his screen name. Between 1929 and 1937 he participated in no less than thirteen Ozu films. David Bordwell called him "diabolical,"[1] and he was indeed very impressive. He also had roles in the films of other directors, and after quitting the screen in 1940, unlike many other child actors, he resumed his career in 1952 and kept appearing on screen regularly until the early 1970's, and occasionally until the final years of his life.

Among his Ozu films four are lost (11, 18, 32, 34) and in two he only had short parts (15, 20). His memorable roles are as follows:

A Straightforward Boy (mostly lost) (1929)

The film from which he adopted his screen name.

I Was Born, But . . . (1932)

Keiji, the younger of the two boys who are disappointed in their father.

1. Bordwell, *Ozu and the Poetics of Cinema*, 249.

Passing Fancy (1933)

Tomio, the son whose trubulent relations with his father are at the heart of the film.

Story of Floating Weeds (1934)

Tomibo, a child actor in the troop.

An Inn in Tokyo (1935)

Zenkō, Kihachi's elder son.

The Only Son (1936)

Tomibo, the neighbor's son who gets kicked by a horse.

What Did the Lady Forget? (1937)

Tomio, the boy who solves an arithmetic problem.

Tōno Eijirō (1907–1994)

In a career lasting over 50 years, he appeared in many hundreds of films, television dramas, and stage production (his final role was in 1990 in Itami Jūzō's *Ageman*), but for Ozu followers he is familiar through his almost identical role in four films, that of the elderly man who while getting drunk expresses his disappointment with life. These roles were as follows:

Tokyo Story (1953)

Numata Sanpei (71), the father's old friend in Tokyo who gets drunk with him and complains about his son's lack of ambition (he was forty-six at the time).

Early Spring (1956)

Hattori Tōkichi, customer in "Blue Mountain," complaining about the life of the *salaryman* and of having no prospects after retirement.

Good Morning (1959)

Tomizawa Hiroshi, retired and looking for a job while often getting drunk, eventually finds one selling electrical goods.

An Autumn Afternoon (1962)

Sakuma Seitaro (72), the old teacher nicknamed "the Gourd," now keeping a cheap restaurant with his unmarried daughter.

Tsukasa Yōko (1934–)

Real name Aizawa Yōko. She was scouted by Ikebe Ryō (see above), becoming an actress in 1954 despite the opposition of her family, and going on to have a long and distinguished career in film and on stage. She had two memorable roles in Ozu's film, as Hara Setsuko's daughter in *Late Autumn* (1960), and as her sister-in-law in *The End of Summer* (1961). She is reputed to have been in continued contact with Hara after the latter retired and secluded herself, until Hara's death.

Wakao Ayako (1933–)

Real name Kurogawa Ayako. She had her debut at eighteen, becoming one of the biggest film stars of her era, appearing in the films of many leading Japanese directors. As she was signed on with Daiei, she appeared in the only film Ozu directed for that studio, *Floating Weeds* (1959), as Kayo, the enchanting younger actress of the traveling actors' troop, who is paid to seduce the son of the troop's head, but soon falls in love with him.

Yamada Isuzu (1917–2012)

Real name Yamada Mitsu. She was born in Osaka into an acting family and debuted in the movies in 1930 aged twelve. Her career in film, television, and on stage lasted until 2001. She was one of the most decorated actresses in Japan, designated Person of Cultural Merit by the Japanese government in 1993, and in 2000 was the first actress to receive the Order of Merit. Her memorable part in an Ozu film was as the estranged mother in *Tokyo Twilight* (1957). She was married four times, and with her first husband Tsukita Ichirō had a daughter, the actress Saga Michiko.

Yamamoto Fujiko (1931–)

She won the first Miss Nippon beauty contest in 1950, and in 1953 was signed on by Daiei Film, appearing in more than one-hundred movies in the following decade. However, in 1963 the studio refused to make the changes she required in her contract, dismissed her, and blocked her participating in any future films made in Japan. She appeared on the stage and in television dramas, but never again on the big screen. Having been born in Osaka and educated in Kyoto, she perfectly fitted the role of Yukiko, the daughter of a traditional Kyoto inn keeper in *Equinox Flower* (1958), who tricks her friend's stubborn father into allowing his daughter to marry the man of her choice.

Yamamura Sō (1910–2000)

Real name Koga Hirosada. Beginning in theatre, he started his film career in 1946, and by 1997 had more than 100 movies to his name, including a few American ones. He also appeared in many television drama series, and directed six films of his own. Yamamura appeared in four Ozu films:

The Munakata Sisters (1950)

Mimura Ryōsuke, the abusive husband who dies in a drunken stupor.

Tokyo Story (1953)

Hirayama Kōichi, the doctor son of the elderly couple.

Early Spring (1956)

Kawai Yutaka, "Blue Mountain" café/bar owner and a friend of the protagonist.

Tokyo Twilight (1957)

Sekiguchi Tsumoru, an old friend of the father.

Yoshikawa Mitsuko (1901–1991)

Real name Yoshikawa Man. Her debut was in 1926, and she was active into the 1970's, appearing in hundreds of films and television dramas. She was one of the two or three most frequent actresses in Ozu's pre-war films, most of which are lost (5, 11, 13, 18, 21, 26, 32), and in one case partially lost (30), but her solid performances, usually as an elegant lady clad in kimono, often a little sarcastic, stand out in several surviving films (20, 24, 35, 36, 37, 39). In 1984 director Itami Jūzō called her back to participate in his first film, *The Funeral*, as he did with several other Ozu regulars in his following movies.

Actors' List

Indicated are the films in which each actor participated, according to the numbers on the attached table of Ozu's films.

Abe Tooru	安部 徹	45	
Aizome Yumeko	逢初夢子	28, 30	
Annan Junko	安南純子	45	
Aoki Hōhi	青木放屁	39, 40, 41	[first name also Tomihiro 富廣]
Aoki Shinobu	青木しのぶ	30	
Aoki Tomio	青木富夫	See: Tokkan Kozō	
Aono Kiyoshi	青野清	31, 32, 34, 35	
Aoyama Mariko	青山万里子	7, 31	
Aratama Michiyo	新珠三千代	52	
Arima Ineko	有馬稲子	47, 48	
Asaji Shinobu	浅茅しのぶ	53	
Asami Hideo	朝海日出男	47	
Atsumi Eiko	渥美映子	1	
Awashima Chikage	淡島千景	43, 44, 46	

Azuma Saburō	吾妻三郎	1	
Bakudan Kozō	爆弾小僧	35, 38	[real name: Yokoyama Jun 横山準]
Benisawa Yōko	紅沢葉子	41	
Chiba Akira	千葉晃	46	
Chichibu Haruko	秩父晴子	45, 47	
Chimura Katsuko	千村克子	52	
Chimura Yōko	千村洋子	46, 47, 48, 49	
Chino Kakuko	千之赫子	51	
Dan Reiko	団玲子	52	
Date Satoko	伊達里子	14, 17, 20, 25, 26	
Date Tadashi	伊達正	50	
Egawa Ureo	江川宇礼雄	25, 27, 48	
Endo Tatsuo	遠藤太津夫	52	
Fujiki Masuo	藤木満寿夫	49	
Fujiki Yū	藤木悠	52	
Fujimatsu Shōtarō	藤松正太郎	24, 38	
Fujimura Yoshiaki	藤村善秋	50	
Fujiwara Kamatari	藤原釜足	42, 47	
Fujino Hideo	藤野秀夫	37	
Fujino Takako	藤乃高子	46	
Fujioka Shōichi	藤丘昇一	44	
Fumiya Chiyoko	文谷千代子	37, 38, 40	
Fushimi Nobuko	伏見信子	29	
Futaba Kaoru	二葉かほる	15, 25	
Hachino Toyoo	蜂野豊夫	8	[read: Toyo-o]

Hanabu Tatsuo	花布辰男	50
Hanaoka Kikuko	花岡菊子	25
Hanayagi Miyako	花柳都	1
Handa Hidemaru	半田日出丸	4
Hara Setsuko	原節子	41, 43, 45, 47, 51, 52
Hara Yoshiko	原順子	51
Hasebe Tomoka	長谷部朋香	43, 44, 46, 47, 51
Hasegawa Masayama	長谷川雅山	48
Hayakawa Kyōji	早川恭二	52
Hayama Masao	葉山正雄	24, 35, 36, 37, 38
Hayami Teruyo	早見照代	24
Hayashi Kuniyasu	林国康	24
Hida Kisao	飛田喜佐夫	50
Higashi Mayumi	東まゆみ	52
Higashiyama Chieko	東山千栄子	43, 45
Higashiyama Mitsuko	東山光子	36
Hikabe Akira	日下部章	34
Hikari Kimiko	光喜三子	19
Himori Shinichi	日守新一	6, 8, 10, 35, 38
Hinatsu Yurie	日夏百合繪	4, 7
Hinatsu Noriko	日夏紀子	44
Hira Yōkō	平陽光	31
Hori Yūji	堀雄二	42
Horikoshi Setsuko	堀越節子	42
Hoshi Hikaru	星ひかる	17, 50

Ichiki Toppa	一木突破	8
Ichimura Mitsuko	市村美津子	16, 18
Ichinomiya Atsuko	一の宮あつ子 42	
Igawa Kuniko	井川邦子	43
Iida Chōko	飯田蝶子	6, 7, 8, 10, 20, 22, 25, 26, 29, 31, 32, 33, 34, 35, 36, 37, 39
Iijima Zentarō	飯島善太郎	24
Iizuka Toshiko	飯塚敏子	20, 21
Ikebe Mitsumura	池部光村	31
Ikebe Ryō	池部良	46
Ikebe Tsurihiko	池部鶴彦	34
Ikumi Aiko	伊久美愛子	47, 48, 51
Imai Kentarō	今井健太郎	46, 47, 48, 53
Inagawa Zenichi	稲川善一	46, 51, 53
Inoue Masahiko	井上正彦	46, 47, 48
Inoue Yukiko	井上雪子	21, 23
Irie Yōsuke	入江洋佑	50
Ishikawa Katsuji	石川克二	47
Ishikawa Kinichi	石川欣一	44
Ishiwatari Teruaki	石渡輝秋	24
Ishiyama Yūji	石山龍児	29, 47
Itō Kazuyo	伊藤和代	43
Itokawa Kazuhiro	糸川和広	45
Itokawa Kyōko	糸川京子	7
Iwashita Shima	岩下志摩	51, 53
Iwata Yukichi	岩田祐吉	30
Izumi Hiroko	泉博子	23

Izumi Keiko	泉啓子	40
Izumi Kyōko	泉京子	49
Izumo Yaeko	出雲八重子	34, 36, 37
Joe Ohara	ジョー・オハラ	50
Kaga Kōji	加賀晃二	28
Kagawa Kyōko	香川京子	45
Kahara Natsuko	賀原夏子	50
Kake Shusuke	懸秀介	31, 32
Kanō Takako	叶多賀子	46
Kashima Shunsaku	鹿島俊作	28
Katō Daisuke	加東大介	46, 52, 53
Katō Seiichi	加藤精一	11, 24, 29, 30, 35
Katsuragi Fumiko	葛城文子	20, 25, 37
Katsuragi Yōko	桂木洋子	41
Kawaguchi Hiroshi	川口浩	50
Kawaguchi Nobu	川口のぶ	46, 47
Kawahara Ken	川原健	52
Kawakane Masanao	川金正直	48
Kawamura Kōhei	川村耿平	48, 51
Kawamura Reikichi	河村黎吉	1, 37, 39, 42
Kawara Kanji	河原 侃二	1, 14, 22, 38
Kawasaki Hiroko	川崎弘子	14, 20, 26
Kimura Kenji	木村健児	6, 10, 14
Kisaragi Teruo	如月輝夫	38
Kishi Keiko	岸恵子	46

Kishida Kyōko	岸田今日子	53	
Kita Ryūji	北竜二	48, 51, 53	
Kitahara Mie	北原三枝	44	
Kiyokawa Akiko	清河晶子	48	
Kobayashi Keiju	小林桂樹	52	
Kobayashi Tokuji	小林十九二	7, 34, 48	
Kofujita Shōichi	小藤田 正一	8, 10, 11, 24, 38	
Kogure Michiyo	木暮実千代	44	
Kojima Kazuko	小島和子	33, 35	
Konami Hatsuko	小波初子	1	[or Onami]
Komachi Kushiro	小町久代	53	
Komaki Kazuko	小牧和子	36	
Kōno Toshiko	河野敏子	37	
Kōno Yūichi	河野祐一	39	
Konoe Toshiaki	近衛敏明	34, 37	
Kozakura Yōko	小桜 葉子	4	
Kozono Yōko	小園容子	44	
Kubota Katsumi	久保田勝巳	38	[or Masami]
Kuga Yoshiko	久我美子	48, 49	
Kuhara Yoshiko	久原良子	36	
Kurata Yūsuke	倉田勇助	38	
Kurishima Sumiko	栗島すみ子	13, 19, 36	
Kuwano Michiko	桑野通子	36, 37	
Kuwano Miyuki	桑野みゆき	48, 51	
Kyō Machiko	京マチ子	50	
Maki Noriko	牧紀子	53	
Marui Tarō	丸井太郎	50	

Maruyama Osamu	丸山修	50	
Masuda Junji	増田順二	46, 47	
Matsui Junko	松井潤子	2, 3, 6, 8, 30	
Matsumura Wakashiro	松村若代	50	
Matsuno Hideo	松野日出夫	46	
Matsuzono Nobuko	松園延子	14	
Mikami Shinichirō	三上真一郎	51, 53	
Miki Takashi	三木隆	45	
Mikura Hiroshi	三倉博	15	
Mimura Hideko	三村秀子	39	
Minakami Reiko	水上令子	40	
Minakata Nobuo	南方伸夫	50	
Minami Yoshie	南美江	51	
Mine Hisako	峰久子	46, 48	
Mishima Masao	三島雅夫	41	
Misumi Hachirō	三角八郎	50	
Mitani Sachiko	三谷幸子	45	
Mito Mitsuko	水戸光子	38	
Mitsui Kōji	三井弘次	28, 30, 31, 38, 40, 46, 50	[also known as 秀男Hideo]
Mitsukawa Kyōko	光川和子	30, 51	[probably two different actresses by the same name]
Miya Sachiko	宮幸子	47	
Miyaguchi Seiji	宮口精二	43, 46, 47	
Miyajima Kenichi	宮島健一	22, 38, 50	

Miyake Kuniko	三宅邦子	37, 41, 43, 44, 45, 46, 49, 51, 53
Miyama Etsuko	美山悦子	44
Miyoshi Eiko	三好栄子	47, 49
Mizuki Ryōko	水木涼子	45
Mizushima Mitsuyo	水島光代	36
Mizushima Ryotarō	水島亮太郎	25
Mizukubo Sumiko	水久保澄子	28
Mochizuki Yūko	望月優子	44, 52
Mori Akiko	森明子	52
Mori Noriko	森教子	47
Mōri Mitsuhiro	毛利充宏	45
Mōri Teruo	毛利輝夫	10, 14, 18, 19
Morikawa Masami	森川まさみ	37
Morishige Hisaya	森繁久彌	52
Morozumi Keijirō	諸角啓二郎	45, 46, 49
Mozuka Morihiko	毛塚守彦	38
Murase Zen	村瀬禅	43, 45, 46
Murata Chieko	村田 知栄子	40
Nagai Tatsurō	永井達郎	38, 46
Nagao Toshinosuke	長尾敏之助	40, 44, 45
Nagaoka Teruko	長岡輝子	45, 46, 47, 48, 49
Nakagawa Hideto	中川秀人	40
Nakagawa Kenzō	中川健三	40
Nakahama Ichizō	中浜一三	5

Nakamura Ganjirō	中村鴈治郎	50, 52
Nakamura Harue	中村はるえ	47
Nakamura Nobuo	中村伸郎	45, 46, 47, 48, 51, 53
Nakakita Chieko	中北千枝子	46
Nakata Tsutomu	中田勉	50
Nakayama Junji	中山淳二	46
Nakayama Sakae	中山さかえ	40
Nangō Yūji	南郷佑児	46
Nanjo Yasuo	南條康雄	20, 28
Naniwa Chieko	浪花千栄子	48, 52
Naniwa Tomoko	浪花友子	5, 7, 9, 19, 35, 36
Nara Shinyō	奈良 真養	13, 21, 26, 27, 30, 38
Nihonyanagi Hiroshi	二本柳寛	43
Niijima Tsutomu	新島勉	45, 47
Nishikawa Tomiko	西川富美子	52
Nishikori Bin	錦織斌	8
Nishimura Seiji	西村青児	24, 26, 28, 29, 31, 33, 37, 38, 39
Nodera Shōichi	野寺正一	1
Nomura Akio	野村秋生	24, 30
Nozoe Hitomi	野添ひとみ	50
Obinata Den	大日方 傳	29, 30
Oda Masao	織田政雄	53
Ogata Shōichi	小勝田正一	38
Ogata Yasuo	緒方安雄	53
Ogawa Kunimatsu	小川国松	1

Ogura Shigeru	小倉繁	2, 3, 8, 19	
Ōizumi Akira	大泉 滉	49	
Oka Jōji	岡譲司	26, 28	
Okada Mariko	岡田茉莉子	51, 53	
Okada Sōtarō	岡田宗太郎	19, 20, 21	
Okada Tokihiko	岡田時彦	16, 19, 20, 21, 22	
Okada Yoshiko	岡田嘉子	26, 27, 33	
Okajima Shōichi	岡島荘一	3	
Okamoto Eiko	岡本エイ子	37	
Okamura Ayako	岡村文子	3, 7	
Okamura Fumiko	岡村文子	13, 37, 40	
Okita Giichi	沖田儀一	38	
Ōkuni Ichirō	大国一朗	5, 8, 9, 15, 18, 19	[name written also: 大邦一公 Ōkuni Ikkō]
Oni Shōsuke	鬼笑介	46, 47, 48, 51	
Osafune Fujiyo	長船フジヨ	39, 40	
Ōsaka Shirō	大坂志郎	45	
Ōsugi Tsuneo	大杉恒雄	38	
Ōta Chieko	太田千恵子	46	
Ōtsuka Kimiyo	大塚君代	36	
Ōtsuka Masayoshi	大塚正義	38	
Ōyama Kenji	大山健二	2, 5, 6, 10, 25, 27, 32, 34, 36, 38	
Ozawa Eitarō	小沢栄太郎	39	

Ryū Chishū	笠智衆	8, 10, 15, 16, 22, 24, 25, 27, 28, 29, 30, 31, 33, 34, 35, 37, 38, 39, 40, 41, 42, 43, 44, 45, 46, 47, 48, 49, 50, 51, 52, 53	
Saburi Shin	佐分利信	37, 38, 44, 48, 51	
Sada Keiji	佐田啓二	48, 49, 51, 53	
Sahara Yasushi	佐原康	46, 47	
Saitō Tatsuo	斉藤達雄	2, 3, 4, 6, 8, 11, 12, 13, 14, 15, 16, 17, 18, 19, 20, 21, 22, 23, 24, 25, 34, 36, 37, 42	
Sakai Saburō	酒井三郎	50	
Sakamoto Takeshi	坂本武	2, 3, 4, 6, 8, 10, 11, 12, 14, 18, 20, 22, 23, 24, 25, 29, 31, 32, 33, 34, 36, 37, 38, 39, 40	
Sakura Mutsuko	桜むつ子	45, 47, 48, 49, 50, 51	
Sano Shūji	佐野周二	36, 38, 40, 43	
Sasaki Masatoki	佐々木正時	50	
Sasaki Tsuneko	佐々木恒子	46, 48	
Satake Akio	佐竹明夫	49	
Satō Michio	佐藤三知雄	24	
Satomi Kenji	里見健児	15	
Sawamura Sadako	沢村貞子	49, 51	
Sazanka Kyū	山茶花究	52	
Segawa Kyōsuke	瀬川恭助	52	
Shiga Matsuko	志賀真津子	43, 44, 53	[first name also written: 直津子]

Seki Tokio	関時男	2, 3, 15, 18
Sengoku Noriko	千石規子	42
Shiho Kyōsuke	志保京助	50
Shimamura Toshio	島村俊雄	46, 47, 49
Shimazu Masahiko	島津雅彦	49, 50, 51, 52
Shimizu Ichirō	清水一郎	40, 41
Shimizu Yoshikazu	清水義和	52
Shin Kinzō	信欣三	47
Shingū Nobuko	新宮信子	50
Shinobu Setsuko	忍節子	37
Shinoyama Masako	篠山正子	47
Shirakawa Yumi	白川由美	52
Shirosawa Isao	城沢勇夫	43
Shirota Hajime	白田肇	49
Shirota Jirō	城多二郎	23
Shirotani Kōji	城谷皓治	47, 51
Shitara Kōji	設楽幸嗣	44, 49, 51
Sono Yukari	園ゆかり	52
Sora Nobuko	空伸子	47, 48
Suematsu Takayuki	末松孝行	33
Suenaga Isao	末永功	46, 47, 48, 51
Suga Fujio	須賀不二男	46, 47, 48, 49, 51, 53
Sugai Ichirō	菅井一郎	43
Sugano Shichirō	菅野七郎	3
Sugawara Hideo	菅原秀雄	22, 24, 29

Sugawara Tsūsai	菅原通済	46, 47, 48, 49, 50, 51, 53	
Sugimori Rin	杉森麟	50	
Sugimura Haruko	杉村春子	41, 43, 45, 46, 47, 49, 50, 52, 53	
Sugita Hiroko	杉田弘子	46	
Sugita Kō	杉田康	50	
Suzuki Shōzō	鈴木彰三	45	
Suzuki Utako	鈴木歌子	10, 14, 36	
Suzuki Yasuyuki	鈴木康之	46	
Tachibana Kazue	橘一枝	48	
Tachibana Mitsuko	橘美津子	52	
Tachibana Yasuko	立花泰子	36	
Takada Minoru	高田稔	10, 13, 14	
Takadō Kuninori	高堂國典	43	
Takagi Mayuko	高木真由子	37	
Takagi Nobuo	高木信夫	47	
Takahashi Teiji	高橋貞二	46, 47, 48	
Takahashi Toyo	高橋とよ	41, 43, 45, 48, 49, 50, 51, 53	[first name also written: 豊, 豊子]
Takamatsu Eiko	高松栄子	2, 8, 9, 35, 39, 40	
Takamine Hideko	高峰秀子	22, 42	
Takamine Mieko	高峰三枝子	37	
Takarada Akira	宝田明	52	
Takasugi Sanae	高杉早苗	34, 42	
Takatori Makiko	鷹取まきこ	52	
Takayama Yoshirō	高山義郎	28	
Takeda Norikazu	竹田法一	46, 48, 49, 51	

Takeda Shunrō	武田春郎	25, 37	[first name also 秀郎 Hiderō, 秀雄 Hideo]
Takemura Nobuo	竹村信夫	28	
Takesato Mitsuko	竹里光子	50	
Takeuchi Ryōichi	竹内良一	32	
Takeuchi Tetsurō	竹内哲郎	50	
Tamaki Miseyo	環三千世	52, 53	
Tanaka Haruo	田中春男	46, 47, 49, 50	
Tanaka Kinuyo	田中絹代	10, 15, 19, 25, 27, 28, 32, 40, 42, 48	
Tani Reikō	谷麗光	22, 23, 28, 29, 31, 37, 38	
Tani Yoshino	谷よしの	39, 40, 43	
Tanizaki Jun	谷崎純	41, 43, 44, 46, 47	
Tashiro Yuriko	田代百合子	51	
Tashiro Yoshiko	田代芳子	43, 45	
Tatsuta Shizue		龍田静枝	13, 19
Taura Masami	田浦正巳	46, 47	
Terada Kayoko	寺田佳代子	43	
Teraoka Kōji	寺岡孝二	47	
Teshirogi Kunio	手代木国男	40	
Toake Hisao	十朱久雄	44, 45, 48, 51	
Tokkan Kozō	突貫小僧	11, 12, 15, 18, 20, 24, 29, 31, 32, 33, 34, 35, 36	[earlier known by real name Aoki Tomio 青木富夫]
Togawa Yoshiko	戸川美子	45	
Tōgō Haruko	東郷晴子	52	
Tōno Eijirō	東野英治郎	45, 46, 49, 53	

Tōyama Fumio	遠山文雄	45
Tonoyama Taiji	殿山泰司	39, 49
Tsubōchi Yoshiko	坪内美子	31, 35, 37, 41, 42
Tsuda Haruhiko	津田晴彦	38
Tsugawa Akemi	津川アケミ	52
Tsujima Keiko	津島恵子	44
Tsukasa Yōko	司葉子	51, 52
Tsukida Ichirō	月田一郎	17, 20
Tsukioka Yumeji	月岡夢路	41
Tsukita Ichirō	月田一郎	15, 18
Tsuruta Kōji	鶴田浩二	44
Uchida Asao	内田朝雄	52
Uehara Ken	上原謙	36, 42
Uehara Yōko	上原葉子	44
Umeka Fumiko	梅香ふみこ	52
Urabe Kumeko	浦辺粂子	46, 47, 50
Usami Jun	宇佐美 淳	41
Ushio Mantarō	潮万太郎	50
Wakaba Nobuko	若葉信子	2, 9
Wakabayashi Hiroo	若林広雄	15
Wakami Takiko	若見多喜子	7
Wakamizu Kinuko	若水絹子	37
Wakamizu Teruko	若水照子	21
Wakamiya Mitsuru	若宮満	31
Wakao Ayako	若尾文子	50

Watanabe Atsushi	渡辺篤	5, 9	
Watanabe Fumio	渡辺文雄	48, 51	
Watanabe Hideto	渡辺秀人	52	
Yagumo Emiko	八雲恵美子	16, 22, 31	[first name also Rieko理恵子]
Yamada Eiko	山田英子	43, 44	
Yamada Fusao	山田房生	8, 15	
Yamada Isuzu	山田五十鈴	47	
Yamada Nagamasa	山田長政	29, 31	
Yamada Yoshikazu	山田好一	46	[Kōichi?]
Yamaguchi Isamu	山口勇	22, 37	
Yamaguchi Ken	山口健	50	
Yamamoto Fujiko	山本富士子	48	
Yamamoto Kazuko	山本和子	46, 47	
Yamamoto Mikiko	山本美紀子	52	
Yamamoto Tami	山本多美	43, 44, 46, 51, 53	
Yamamoto Tōgō	山本冬郷	16, 19	
Yamamura Sō	山村聡	42, 45, 46, 47	
Yamashina Yukari	山科ゆかり	51	
Yamayoshi Kōsaku	山吉鴻作	47	
Yanagi Eijirō	柳永二郎	44	
Yokoo Dekao	横尾泥海男	15, 19	
Yokoyama Gorō	横山五郎	15	
Yokoyama Jun	横山準	See: Bakudan Kozō 爆弾小僧	

Yoshida Teruo	吉田輝雄	53
Yoshikawa Masae	吉川雅恵	52
Yoshikawa Mitsuko	吉川満子	5, 11, 13, 18, 20, 21, 24, 26, 30, 32, 35, 36, 37, 39
Yoshitani Hisao	吉谷久雄	2, 9, 14
Yui Munenobu	油井宗信	31
Yūki Ichirō	結城 一朗	8, 9
Yūki Michiyo	結城三千代	52

Table of Ozu's Films

1	*Sword of Penitence*	懺悔の刃 *Zange no yaiba*	1927	B&W, silent	lost
2	*The Dreams of Youth*	若人の夢 *Wakōdo no yume*	1928	B&W, silent	lost
3	*Wife Lost*	女房紛失 *Nyōbō funshitsu*	1928	B&W, silent	lost
4	*Pumpkin*	カボチャ *Kabocha*	1928	B&W, silent	lost
5	*A Couple on the Move*	引越し夫婦 *Hikkoshi fūfu*	1928	B&W, silent	lost
6	*Body Beautiful*	肉体美 *Nikutaibi*	1928	B&W, silent	lost
7	*Treasure Mountain*	宝の山 *Takara no yama*	1929	B&W, silent	lost
8	*Days of Youth*	若き日 *Wakaki hi*	1929	B&W, silent	
9	*Fighting Friends – Japanese Style*	和製喧嘩友達 *Wasei kenka tomodachi*	1929	B&W, silent	mostly lost
10	*I Graduated, But . . .*	大学は出たけれど *Daigaku wa detakeredo*	1929	B&W, silent	mostly lost
11	*The Life of an Office Worker*	会社員生活 *Kaishain seikatsu*	1929	B&W, silent	lost

12	*A Straightforward Boy*	突貫小僧 *Tokkan kozō*	1929	B&W, silent	mostly lost
13	*An Introduction to Marriage*	結婚学入門 *Kekkongaku nyūmon*	1930	B&W, silent	lost
14	*Walk Cheerfully*	朗かに歩め *Hogarakani ayume*	1930	B&W, silent	
15	*I Flunked, But . . .*	落第はしたけれど *Rakudai wa shita keredo*	1930	B&W, silent	
16	*That Night's Wife*	その夜の妻 *Sono yo no tsuma*	1930	B&W, silent	
17	*The Revengeful Spirit of Eros*	エロ神の怨霊 *Erogami no onryō*	1930	B&W, silent	lost
18	*Lost Luck*	足に触った幸運 *Ashi ni sawatta kōun*	1930	B&W, silent	lost
19	*Young Miss*	お嬢さん *Ojōsan*	1930	B&W, silent	lost
20	*The Lady and the Beard*	淑女と髭 *Shukujo to hige*	1931	B&W, silent	
21	*Beauty's Sorrows*	美人哀愁 *Bijin aishū*	1931	B&W, silent	lost
22	*Tokyo Chorus*	東京の合唱 *Tōkyō no gasshō*	1931	B&W, silent	
23	*Spring Comes from the Ladies*	春は御婦人から *Haru wa gofujin kara*	1932	B&W, silent	lost
24	*I Was Born, But . . .*	生れてはみたけれど *Umarete wa mita keredo*	1932	B&W, silent	
25	*Where Now Are the Dreams of Youth?*	青春の夢いまいづこ *Seishun no yume ima izuko*	1932	B&W, silent	
26	*Until the Day We Meet Again*	また逢ふ日まで *Mata au hi made*	1932	B&W, silent	lost
27	*Woman of Tokyo*	東京の女 *Tōkyō no onna*	1933	B&W, silent	

28	*Dragnet Girl*	非常線の女 *Hijōsen no onna*	1933	B&W, silent	
29	*Passing Fancy*	出来ごころ *Dekigokoro*	1933	B&W, silent	
30	*A Mother Should Be Loved*	母を恋わずや *Haha o kowazu ya*	1934	B&W, silent	parts lost
31	*Story of Floating Weeds*	浮草物語 *Ukigusa monogatari*	1934	B&W, silent	
32	*An Innocent Maid*	箱入り娘 *Hakoiri musume*	1935	B&W, silent	lost
33	*An Inn in Tokyo*	東京の宿 *Tōkyō no yado*	1935	B&W, part sound	
34	*College is a Nice Place*	大学よいとこ *Daigaku yoi toko*	1936	B&W, part sound	lost
35	*The Only Son*	ひとり息子 *Hitori musuko*	1936	B&W	
36	*What Did the Lady Forget?*	淑女は何を忘れたか *Shukujo wa nani o wasureta ka*	1937	B&W	
37	*The Brothers and Sisters of the Toda Family*	戸田家の兄 *Todake no kyōdai*	1941	B&W	
38	*There was a Father*	父ありき *Chichi ariki*	1942	B&W	
39	*Record of a Tenement Gentleman*	長屋紳士録 *Nagaya shinshiroku*	1947	B&W	
40	*A Hen in the Wind*	風の中の牝鶏 *Kaze no naka no mendori*	1948	B&W	
41	*Late Spring*	晩春 *Banshun*	1949	B&W	
42	*The Munakata Sisters*	宗方姉妹 *Munakata shimai*	1950	B&W	
43	*Early Summer*	麦秋 *Bakushū*	1951	B&W	
44	*The Flavor of Green Tea over Rice*	お茶漬けの味 *Ochazuke no aji*	1952	B&W	

45	*Tokyo Story*	東京物語 *Tōkyō monogatari*	1953	B&W
46	*Early Spring*	早春 *Shoshun*	1956	B&W
47	*Tokyo Twilight*	東京暮色 *Tōkyō boshoku*	1957	B&W
48	*Equinox Flower*	彼岸花 *Higanbana*	1958	Color
49	*Good Morning*	お早よう *Ohayō*	1959	Color
50	*Floating Weeds*	浮草 *Ukigusa*	1959	Color
51	*Late Autumn*	秋日和 *Akibiyori*	1960	Color
52	*The End of Summer*	小早川家の秋 *Kohayakawake no aki*	1961	Color
53	*An Autumn Afternoon*	秋刀魚の味 *Sanma no aji*	1962	Color

Fully lost: 17 films
Mostly lost: 3 films
Partially lost: 1 film
Surviving: 32 films (13 silent, 19 talkies)

Select Bibliography, Annotated

A LARGE BODY OF studies concerning Ozu's cinema has accumulated since the 1970's in English, and a much wider literature of various kinds has been published in Japanese. The following is a selection of books I have used in writing this one, or found of special interest, arranged in order of publication under each language.

English

Donald Richie. *Ozu*. Berkeley: University of California Press, 1974.

[The ground-breaking book about Ozu, by the man who was almost single-handedly responsible for introducing his films to the world outside Japan.]

Audie Bock. *Japanese Film Directors*. Tokyo: Kodansha, 1978.

[The cinema of ten Japanese auteurs is examined by a scholar well familiar with the scene, including a valuable chapter on Ozu.]

David Bordwell. *Ozu and the Poetics of Cinema*. Princeton University Press, 1988.

[The seminal study of Ozu's cinematic technic and sensibilities, a book into which anyone genuinely wishing to understand the director's work should delve again and again.]

David Desser, ed. *Ozu's Tokyo Story*. Cambridge Film Handbooks, Cambridge University Press, 1997.

[A useful introduction to Ozu's most famous film through articles by various authors, and with some addenda.]

Shinnosuke Kometani. *Chasing Ozu*. Translated by Kimiko Takeda. Tokyo: The Publishing Arts Institute, 2021.

[A translation of a personal view of Ozu's films by a Japanese author, with some interesting information and observations.]

Japanese

佐藤忠男『小津安二郎の芸術』朝日新聞社　1971.

[This book by Japan's most distinguished film scholar, was later published in other editions, including with a new afterword in 2000, and a second printing in 2004.]

佐藤忠男監修『永遠のマドンナ原節子のすべて』出版協同社　1986.

[A book about actress Hara Setsuko detailing her career, including a great number of photographs and some memories from those who knew her.]

『小津安二郎を読む』本の映画館ブック・シニマテーク—5、フィルムアート社　1982.

[A very useful book containing detailed information on each of the films and on various aspects of Ozu's life and work.]

厚田雄春／蓮實重彦『小津安二郎物語』ルミエル叢書1 筑摩書房　1989.

[A book written as a dialogue between Atsuta Yūharu, Ozu's cinematographer, and Tokyo University professor Hasumi Shigehiko, with a great number of photographs.]

『小津安二郎集城』キネマ旬報特別編集　1989; 1992.

[A book containing parts of Ozu's diary, articles by various people close to him, and reviews from *Kinema Jumpo* magazine.]

笠智衆『大船日記一小津安二郎先生の思い出』扶桑社　1991.

[A short memoire by actor Ryū Chishū, mostly about acting for Ozu but also about his later work, with a list of more than 300 films in which he appeared.]

『いま、小津安二郎』Shotor Library　小学館　2003.

[A short book containing some memories of Ozu, an article about clothes in his films, his accessories, his favorite restaurants, and more, with many photographs.]

井上和男編『小津安二郎全集上、下』新書館　2003–2004.

[The extant scripts of Ozu's films, some reconstructions of the films lost without a script, and his scripts given to other directors, in two beautifully printed volumes.]

Japanese & English

『デジタル小津安二郎編　―キャメラマン厚田雄春の視―』 / *From Behind the Camera: A New Look at the World of Director Yasujiro Ozu – Based on Private Materials of the Late Yuharu Atsuta –* Edited by Ken Sakamura and Shigehiko Hasumi, Tokyo University Digital Museum, 1998.

[Contains Japanese material, large parts of which are also translated into English, with beautiful color photography (exhibition catalogue).]

『小津安二郎映画読本』/ *Yasujiro Ozu: Japanese Film Master*
フィルムアート社　1993; 2004.

[A useful booklet in Japanese, with a digest in English of the short articles on each film. Issued as a catalogue for a retrospective on Ozu's 100th anniversary.]

www.ingramcontent.com/pod-product-compliance
Lightning Source LLC
LaVergne TN
LVHW050635100826
845148LV00011B/1868

* 9 7 9 8 3 8 5 2 7 8 8 6 2 *